JOURNAL FOR THE STUDY OF THE OLD TESTAMENT
SUPPLEMENT SERIES
34

Editors
David J.A. Clines
Philip R. Davies

Department of Biblical Studies
The University of Sheffield
Sheffield S10 2TN
England

THE
TEMPLE
SCROLL

An Introduction, Translation & Commentary

Johann Maier

Journal for the Study of the Old Testament
Supplement Series 34

To the Memory of
Yigael Yadin

First published in German in 1978 by Ernst Reinhardt Verlag, Munich
English translation by Richard T. White

Published by
JSOT Press
Department of Biblical Studies
The University of Sheffield
Sheffield S10 2TN
England

Printed in Great Britain
by Redwood Burn Ltd.,
Trowbridge, Wiltshire.

British Library Cataloguing in Publication Data

Maier, Johann
    The temple scroll.—(Journal for the
    study of the Old Testament supplement series,
    ISSN 0309-0787; 34)
    1. Temple scroll—Commentaries
    I. Title   II. Die Tempelrolle vom Toten Meer.
    English   III. Series
    221.4'4   BM488.T44

    ISBN 1-85075-003-3
    ISBN 1-85075-004-1 Pbk

CONTENTS

FOREWORD

Towards the end of 1977 Yigael Yadin published the longest of the Qumran scrolls known so far. The existence of this scroll, which he called the Temple Scroll, had been known since 1960 when a Bethlehem antiquities dealer offered it for sale through agents abroad but negotiations were protracted until 1967. After Israeli troops occupied Bethlehem during the Six Day War, Yadin, with military assistance, tracked down the scroll at the antiquities dealer's house and on the basis of Jordanian law confiscated it. Yadin later announced that the dealer had been paid $105,000 compensation. Thus it appears that the way in which the scroll came into Israeli hands was also technically legal.

Since 1967 the scholarly world has eagerly awaited the publication of this text about which only the most meagre evidence had become available. To a large extent the long delay can be attributed to the poor state of the scroll's preservation. This obviously presented great difficulties so far as opening, preserving and deciphering were concerned. Thanks to a wide variety of photographic techniques it was possible to arrive at a degree of legibility which, in view of the condition of the scroll, is remarkable even though this can be achieved only by constant reference to all the photographs prepared. Yadin was not content merely to publish the text; he also provided an extensive commentary and an additional volume analyzing the more important themes found in the scroll; the work was published first in modern Hebrew. Details are as follows:

Yigael Yadin, *Megillat ham-Miqdas. The Temple Scroll* (Hebrew Edition), Jerusalem (Israel Exploration Society/Hebrew University-Institute of Archaeology) 1977, Vol. I-IIIa.

Vol. I. Introduction, xx and 308 pp. dealing mainly with the festivals and the cultic calendar, purity laws, plan of the Temple, royal authority and hanging (crucifixion) as the death penalty.

Vol. II. Text and Commentary, x and 323 pp. This volume contains a restored text with extensive notes; from p. 231 a more fully reconstructed version of the text; pp. 275ff. a concordance and finally an index of passages quoted: p. 303ff. Old Testament; pp. 313ff. the Samaritan text tradition and ancient versions of the Bible; p. 314 Apocrypha and Pseudepigrapha; p. 315f. Qumran texts; p. 317 Philo and Josephus; p. 318 New Testament; pp. 318-22 Talmudic literature; p. 322f. Maimonides, *Mishneh Torah* and Joseph Karo, *Shulhan Arukh*.

Vol. III. Plates and Texts, viii and 82 plates. Photographs of the columns with a transcription on the facing page.

Vol. IIIa. Supplementary Plates, 40 plates. Mainly additional photographs of columns using various photographic techniques, particularly of the 'mirror image' text from the back of a number of columns (here reproduced in reverse)—because the scroll was so firmly stuck together text was transferred to the back of a number of parts of the scroll. In addition photographs of several fragments of other copies of the text from the Rockerfeller Museum are included.

The English edition, announced for 1978, was delayed for a considerable time and Yadin was not able to produce it until shortly before his death:

The Temple Scroll, edited by Yigael Yadin, Jerusalem 1983.
    Vol. I—Introduction
    Vol. II—Text and Commentary
    Vol. III & IIIa have been taken over from the first edition.

As the Bibliography shows, since the initial publication in 1977 comparatively little has been published to take the discussion further. In the English version Yadin took into consideration a number of new readings but made only slight alterations in content. In the Appendix to Vol. I, pp. 405ff., he offered a concise discussion of the relevant secondary literature. In this section (p. 414f.) he also tackles the question of the lay-out of the Temple. Basically he adhered to his original point of view and leaves a final decision to await further discussion. The English revision does not seem to have been made consistently for there are certain contradictions in statements made about the dimensions of the courts.

The English translation offered here had already been completed when Yadin's English version appeared but it was still possible to take it into consideration—partly at the manuscript stage and partly at the proof stage. The reader will find the page numbers of Yadin's English edition added in italics and brackets to the page numbers of the Hebrew edition. There will also be found an indication of the major differences from the first edition. For the rest the English translation was made on the basis of a revised version of the German translation *Die Tempelrolle vom Toten Meer*. The notes have been expanded to incorporate the most important opinions of the secondary literature that has appeared so far. But the overriding aim was the same as for the previous edition: to present a readable translation as faithful to the text as possible, with concise annotations.

In one basic point the content of the English edition differs from the German. In the latter I preferred the minimal solution for the Temple layout. After careful consideration and further analysis of Yadin's arguments the maximal solution now seems to me to be simpler. In this respect the difference between my opinions and those of Yadin has increased somewhat. The remaining alterations are restricted to a number of different readings without substantial change in content.

The translation has been made on the basis of such text as can be read from the photographs (for this purpose all the photographs including, of course, those in Vol. IIIa have to be taken into consideration). Textual restorations have been taken over only sparingly (even where Yadin feels that they are certain) in order to prevent readers with no knowledge of Hebrew from reaching doubtful conclusions.

At first glance reading the translation is not easy. The first third of the scroll is unfortunately badly damaged and in parts it is extremely difficult to read. Furthermore, the contents, particularly with regard to the Temple, are not easy to understand. It is therefore recommended that the list of contents in the Introduction (pp. 8-19) be studied first, then the appropriate preliminary remarks, which can be found in the notes, on the major themes of the text.

Finally I should like to extend cordial thanks to Philip R. Davies and JSOT Press both for their interest in producing this English edition and for their efforts to that end. I should also like to express particular thanks to the translator, Richard White, who has applied his knowledge of the subject matter and his energies to producing a suitable English version.

Johann Maier
Bruhl, December 1984

ABBREVIATIONS

JQR	*Jewish Quarterly Review*
JBL	*Journal of Biblical Literature*
VT	*Vetus Testamentum*
ET	*Expository Times*
RB	*Revue Biblique*
HUCA	*Hebrew Union College Annual*
RQ	*Revue de Qumran*
DJD	*Discoveries in the Judaean Desert*
BASOR	*Bulletin of the American Schools of Oriental Research*
ZAW	*Zeitschrift für die alttestamentliche Wissenschaft*
BA	*Biblical Archeologist*
IEJ	*Israel Exploration Journal*
Yadin I-III	Y. Yadin, מגילת־המקדש, Jerusalem, 1978
I-III	Y. Yadin, *The Temple Scroll*, Jerusalem, 1984

INTRODUCTION

1. *The Scroll*

The Scroll is made up of 19 pieces of comparatively thin leather and evidently, even when in use, needed repair in a number of places. Indeed, it had been partially replaced at the beginning, for the first piece of leather, containing the text of columns 2–4, was written on by a later scribe (A) with the result that the text of column 5 overlaps somewhat with that of column 6. Since the beginning of the scroll is lost, Yadin begins his numbering of the columns with 2. The end of the text is also missing, as the scribe did not finish writing on the scroll; a blank space follows the beginning of a sentence at the end of column 66.

It is the upper part of the scroll which has suffered most damage. However, at the time of recovery columns 2–5 and 6–8 were also completely stuck together in bundles so that opening, preserving, and deciphering them was unusually difficult. So firmly were they attached that—as occurred in the later columns also—there was extensive loss of text. Nevertheless, because the scroll was rolled up, the text has been partially preserved as a mirror image on the reverse of the adjacent piece of leather and a partial reading is possible, albeit back to front. Because of uneven shrinking the leather has been considerably distorted and so one must contend with a degree of uncertainty. It is really only the last third of the scroll which, not least because of excellent photographs, is comparatively easy to read and most substantially preserved. The overall length of the preserved parts amounts to 9 metres, of which 8.75 metres have been written on (compare 1QIsaᵃ, which is 7.34 metres). The text as we have it consists of 66 columns, each of which (probably) contained 22 lines until column 48, and thereafter 28 lines.

2. *Script and Dating*

It is clear that there were several copies of at least parts of the text; the fragments from the Rockefeller Museum, which Yadin has published in Vol. IIIA, prove this beyond doubt. The main part of the scroll, written by Scribe B, corresponds to the Middle Herodian Ornamental script (dated to the turn of the eras), while the replacement part, columns 2–5 (Scribe A), is Late Herodian and thus from a somewhat later period. Among the fragments from the Rockefeller Museum, No. 43.366 probably comes from the period between 125 and 100 BCE. Hence the original date of composition must be earlier than this.

3. *Orthography and Language*

The orthography and grammar correspond to the forms and usages of the other Qumran texts. Numerous examples of fuller suffix forms and full (non-reduced) syllables in verb forms are attested. The new scroll is also of interest for its syntax and particularly for its use of the 'tenses'.

Where it departs from the wording of the biblical text and rewrites biblical material, the language of the Temple Scroll at the final stage of its redaction can be identified as late Ancient Hebrew, an observation consistent with the palaeographic evidence. However, the idiom of the non-Biblical parts follows Biblical Hebrew. Whether we are dealing, in any particular instance, with an intentionally archaizing style or with features of a more ancient tradition requires further investigation (for the present see G. Brin, *Leshonenu* 43, 20-28).

From the lexicographical point of view the following instances merit attention:

ארב or ארב, 24.8 (cf. *ad loc.*)
רשך, 41.16: 'post'
דלת, 33.13 as a verb in the *pu'al* participle: 'provide with doors'
יום הברכה, 29.8-10 for the eschaton
ראוי ל . . . , 63.9: 'permissible to'
רובד, 4.4f.; 46.5 'ledge, cornice, step, terrace'.

In addition, the meaning of some familiar words is made clearer:

אזרוע/זרוע: 'thigh of foreleg' as opposed to:
שכם: 'shoulder', as part of the sacrificial animals
יצהר: 'fresh oil'
פרור: a porch open to one side, perhaps a sort of stoa or (if columns are assumed) a peristyle
תירוש: 'new wine' ('current vintage').

It is noteworthy that no Greek influence can be detected, not even in technical architectural vocabulary.

4. *Relationship to the Traditional Bible Text*

The Temple Scroll provides the Biblical scholar with scope for research and discussion especially because of the form of the Biblical texts contained in it. Many biblical quotations appear in a modified, abbreviated or expanded form and it is not uncommon to find several Biblical passages which deal with similar subject matter, merged together in both form and content. Such tendentious alterations do imply *a priori* a text form that is divergent from the late 'Masoretic text'.

The most immediately striking feature is that the Temple Scroll almost invariably alters third person to first person when recording divine revelations from the Biblical text. This is virtually always the case when the use of the third person in passages from Deuteronomy might call into question the non-mediated character of the revelation. However, non-biblical parts of the Temple Scroll are also set out as direct divine speech (in the first person) addressed to Moses and are thus presented as containing 'Torah'.

The largest part of the Scroll deals with provisions for the building of the Temple after the conquest of the Land and for the organization of the cult, thus filling an obvious gap in the Pentateuch. It is immediately apparent that we are dealing here with concerns which are peculiar to the Qumran community and which would thus be authorized as direct divine revelation—as 'Torah'—from Sinai. Moreover, since Biblical passages (dealing with festivals and sacrifices) have been woven together, they should not be treated first and foremost as textual witnesses but rather as modified and adapted Biblical material.

Nevertheless, the Temple Scroll does present us with an exciting document from the point of view of textual history. Although much can be attributed to the redactional reworking mentioned above and to the sectarian bias which we have just indicated, yet a distinct closeness to the Greek translation (the Septuagint) can at times be detected. That is to say, in such cases, the exemplar that was used stands closer to the *Vorlage* of the Septuagint than to the Masoretic (traditional Hebrew) text. Whether such an exemplar can be regarded as a 'vulgar' text must remain an open question, but it must surely be counted among the many early text traditions that existed within the various divisions of early Judaism. The exemplar of the Torah which lies behind the Septuagint was probably a text that corresponded to the standard text in the Jerusalem Temple. The Qumran community, which was under priestly influence, doubtless continued to maintain such a tradition. At this juncture the question arises whether there were such things as published and unpublished Bible texts, and of such a sort as to lead in the course of time to differing published versions. If this is so, then one may ask how much more the unpublished texts might possibly have contained than the published versions—a question of particular significance for the text of Ezekiel. It must, of course, be borne in mind that for the compilers or redactors of the Temple Scroll the text-form seemed to be less important than the content or meaning. In this connection the reworking of Biblical material by Flavius Josephus in his *Jewish Antiquities* is particularly instructive, in that he claims to provide a correct and complete repetition of the text (*Ant.* 1.17). In Yadin's opinion, and that of others, the distinctive elements in the Temple Scroll all bear witness to the sectarian inclinations of the Qumran community and, on those rare occasions when he attributes them to the existence of an older underlying text, he plays down the significance of the deviation. But in fact it is scarcely credible that all these cultic prescriptions originated simply from an attitude opposed to the practices of the Temple in Jerusalem at the time. Although much may be laid to the account of contemporary polemics, the majority of these prescriptions must have an older origin—namely from the Zadokite cultic tradition before the troubles at the beginning of the 2nd century BCE.

Such cultic prescriptions scarcely had any greater authority than that of statutes formulated by human beings, yet within the Zadokite priesthood they were more likely to have been seen as containing revelation. Were they intended only for internal use and hence never issued publicly? This question will have to be examined thoroughly. In the meantime, quotations of the Biblical text have been investigated principally by G. Brin (*Shnaton* 4, 182-225). Admittedly, he takes as his starting point the notion that the Masoretic text (*sic!*) was a necessary prerequisite for the 'author' of the Temple Scroll and that all deviations from it can be attributed to the particular sectarian interests of this Qumranic 'author'. The matter is probably more complicated, and bound up with the literary history of the scroll— which is itself far from simple. In the framework of this lightly annotated translation it is not possible to offer a detailed comparison between the text of the Temple Scroll and the Biblical text. But anyone who wishes to follow up the more important deviations in content can find the most obvious examples by using the following survey of contents and the Biblical passages indicated there. Naturally, caution must be exercised: here and there the familiar Bible versions differ considerably from the translations of particular Biblical passages that we offer here, even when the Hebrew text is completely or virtually identical. The reason for this lies in the interpretation of the text, for within the framework of the Temple Scroll we must, wherever possible, follow the meaning of the text *at the time in question* and not a modern translation. In this respect too, detailed research is required.

5. *The General Character of the Work*

At first sight the contents of the scroll, particularly in the last part, seem somewhat disparate. But it is in fact a well thought out composition which is set out in such a way as to correspond to the hierarchy of areas of holiness distinguished in the cultic conceptions of the time, and not only at Qumran. These featured a notion of concentric areas of holiness, increasing in their degree of holiness from zone to zone and culminating in the Holy of Holies—the place of the presence of God.

In ascending order of priority, from the outside inwards, the areas of holiness are as follows:

1. The Holy Land
    a. the city
    b. the building
2. An area around the Holy City, the distance of a three days' journey
3. A zone of 3 *ris* (about 4 miles) around the Holy City
4. The Holy City
5. The Temple Mount
6. The outer Temple court, open to all ritually pure Israelites of both sexes
7. The area for men who are cultically qualified
8. The priests' area (forbidden to laymen)
9. The outer area for cult worship around the altar for burnt-offerings and the Temple building
10. The inner area for cult worship (*hêkāl*), the hall of the Temple, with incense altar, shewbread table and candelabrum

11.   The innermost area for cult worship, the Holy of Holies, the
      place of the presence of God

In the first chapter of *Kelim*, the Mishnah contains a similar list of
areas of holiness. But the Temple Scroll does not proceed in the
manner just described, from outside inward; rather it sees everything
from the priestly point of view and thus is constantly looking from
the *inside* to the *outside*. As a result, the text begins with the
treatment of the Temple, its cult and the arrangement of its courts,
proceeds to stipulations about the Holy City and finishes with laws of
a more general application. Hence 'Holiness Scroll' would really be a
more appropriate name than 'Temple Scroll', especially since the
basic concern of the text is to divide carefully between the areas of
holiness. With respect to the Temple enclosure this is achieved also
by its architectural layout (see the introductions to the relevant
sections in the notes). Within this framework the Temple Scroll has
adapted the relevant biblical traditions, expanded or shortened them
and brought them together into a unified statement. In fact, in the
latter part of the Scroll this almost achieves the form of a codification
and for this reason it has been decided to divide the list of contents
into paragraphs (§). The entire content of the Scroll appears as direct
revelation from God to Moses on Sinai, starting after Exodus 34. It
could be said that the Scroll goes beyond Deuteronomy in its
pseudepigraphic character insofar as a sort of 'Ur-deuteronomy' is
presented here, i.e. the substance of divine speech direct to Moses,
which Moses reports only later in Deuteronomy itself, at a later time
shortly before the conquest of the land.

Anyone who approaches the Temple Scroll with a fixed notion of
canonicity will find this technique audacious. Such a state of affairs
will doubtless stimulate renewed discussion of the emergence of the
canon and the concept of canonicity at that time, even though the
book of Jubilees, with whose contents the Scroll shows substantial
contact, already attests a similar phenomenon.

In his recent book, *The Dawn of Qumran*, B.Z. Wacholder has
attempted to set the Temple Scroll fully in the general context of
Qumran. In his opinion it contains a Qumran alternative to the
Torah from Sinai—so to speak an eschatological Torah. Similarly,
the plan of the Temple would indicate the Temple for the final days
(see cols. 29ff.) which, for the Qumran community, had already
begun. The author of the Scroll is claimed to be the Teacher of
Righteousness and is identified with the Zadok of CD 4.1 (d. 170

BCE). The plan of the Temple is allegedly based on Ex. 25ff., and not on Ezek. 40ff. and similar models. Unfortunately, this bold theory is encumbered with erroneous suppositions, particularly with regard to the views of Yadin, so that a substantial part of the book's polemic is really superfluous. The details of the connections with the halachic traditions of early Jewish and later literature are interesting; but here too the diatribe against Yadin is unnecessary and ill-founded.

THE CONTENTS OF THE TEMPLE SCROLL

TRANSLATION

[ ]	restoration
. . .	text missing or illegible
(*italic*)	explanatory notes or references
(roman)	words added to clarify the sense
{ }	additions made in the Scroll itself
< >	conjectural emendations
° °	restored from additional fragments

Column 2

¹ . . . [for it is terrible what] I will d[o to you] . . . ² . . . [Behold I will drive out before you] the A[morites], . . . ³ . . . ites and the Per[izzites], . . . ⁴ [Jebusites (*Ex. 34.11*). Ta]ke heed for yourself, lest you make a cove[nant with the inhabitants of the land,] ⁵ [to whom you] are coming, so that they do not become a sn[are in your (?) midst] (*Ex. 34.12*), ⁶ [rather] their [altar]s you shall tear down and [their] *mazzeboth* [you shall smash] ⁷ [and t]heir [*asherim*] you shall cut down (*Ex. 34.13*). And the statues of [their] god[s you shall burn] ⁸ [with fire (*LXX; cf. Dt. 7.25*)]. You shall [n]ot covet silver and gold (*Dt. 7.25*), wh[ich] . . . ⁹ . . . You shall [not] take it from him (*cf. Dt. 7.25*) and you shall not br[ing it as an abomination into your house,] ¹⁰ [and thus become] an accursed thing like it. You shall utterly detest [it and you shall utterly abhor it], ¹¹ [for] it is an accursed thing (*Dt. 7.26*). And you shall not bow down before any [other] go[d for YHWH is jealous] ¹² [by name], he is a jealous god (*Ex. 34.14*). Take heed for yourself lest you make [a covenant with the inhabitants of the land]; ¹³ [for they run] after [their] go[ds and] slaughter offerings to [their gods] . . . (*Ex. 34.15*) ¹⁴⁻¹⁵ (*only insignificant remains of letters from Ex. 34.15-16*).

Column 3

¹ . . . which . . . ² . . . violet-purple wool and red-purple wool . . . ³ . . . [al]l your enemies . . . ⁴ . . . [hou]se, in order to s[e]t my (*his ?*) name upon it . . . ⁵ . . . in it silver and gold from all l[ands (?)] . . . ⁶ . . . and you shall not make it impure but by . . . ⁷ . . . [bron]ze and iron and

hewn stone, to b[uild] ... ^{8} ... And all its vessels they shall make from pu[re] ... gold ^{9} ... cover which is over it pure gold ... ^{10} ... [fr]agrant incense and the tab[le] ... ^{11} ... the bowl shall never move from the sanctuary ... ^{12} ... and its sprinkling bowls shall be of pure gold and [its] fire holder[s] ... ^{13} ... [to] bring fire inside with them. And the candelabrum and ... ^{14} ... and the entire altar for burnt-offe[rings ... ^{15} ... [bron]ze pure and the grating (?) wh[ich] is over ... ^{16} ... bronze ... to see ... ^{17} ... [bro]nze, bronze (?) ... ^{18} ...

Column 4

^{1} ... ^{2} ... emerge to ... ^{3} ... are wide fo[ur (?)] ... ^{4} ... and a terrace {is} between the ... ^{5} ... the sixth, a terrace ... ^{6} ... ^{7} ... the width. And the height of the ... ^{8} ... And you shall build (*or 'divide'* *or 'enter'*) the porch ... ^{9} ... ten cubits. And (the) walls ... ^{10} ... and height sixty cubi[ts] ... ^{11} ... [t]welve cubits ... ^{12} ... twenty-one cubits ... ^{13} ... twenty cubits square ... ^{14} ... ^{15} ... its half (?) ... $^{16-17}$ ...

Column 5

^{1} ... joined ... ^{2} ... cubits ... ^{3} ... [th]ickness thr[ee] ... ^{4} ... according to the measure ... ^{5} ... of twen[ty]-eight ^{6} ... and (the) timberwork also ^{7} ... cubits is the total height. ^{8} ... and four gates ^{9} ... of the gate twelve ^{10} ... cubits. And the whole framewo[rk] ^{11} ... [lo]wer and everything overlaid ^{12} ... ^{13} ... And you shall make ... a porch ... ^{14} ... in all ...

Column 6

From here Scribe B

^{1} ... ^{2} ... over ... ^{3} ... cubits ... ^{4} ... ^{5} ... ten cubits is the total height of the framework and ... ^{6} ... gates to the upper chamber to four ... ^{7} ... twelve (?) ... one ... ^{8} ... its doors (?) ... the lower and everything ... ^{9} ...

Column 7

$^{0-1}$ ... ^{2} ... not ... ^{3} ... boards of wo[od] ... ^{4} ... cubits and ten ...

⁵ ... eighty bo[ards (?)] ... ⁶ ... over all ... ⁷ ... hundred (?) ...
⁸ ... in total five cub[its (?)] ... ⁹ ... its height. And the cover which
is ab[ove] ... ¹⁰ ... its width and two cherubim ... ¹¹ ... the other
end extend wings (?) ... ¹² ... above the ark and their faces ...
¹³ ... And you shall make a curtain of gold ... ¹⁴ ... [a]rtistic
wor[k] ... the curt[ain]. ¹⁵ (*illegible remains*)

Column 8

¹⁻² ... ³ ... and seven (?) ... ⁴ ... ⁵ ... and one cubit ... ⁶ ... and
you shall make ... ⁷ ... ⁸ ... two ... ⁹ ... above the two rows
¹⁰ ... this incense to the bread to ... ¹¹ ... incense altar at y[our (?)]
removing ¹² ... bread, you shall put incense on it. Not ¹³ ... et[er-
(?)]nal for their generations and ... this ¹⁴ ... shall come ...

Column 9

¹⁻² ... ³ ... from its two sides ⁴ ... on the one (side) three ⁵ ... and
its knobs ... ⁶⁻⁷ ... ⁸ ... three ⁹ ... the entire shaft ¹⁰ ... these (?)
three ¹¹ ... and its snuffers altogether (two) talents ¹² [of pure gold
(?)] ... all its lamps and you shall give ¹³ ... And the priests, the
sons of ... shall prepare ¹⁴ ... as statutes for ev[er] for their [gener-
ations]

Column 10

¹⁻⁷ (*only very slight remains*) ⁸ ... gate shall be ... ⁹ ... above the
gate ¹⁰ ... crimson ¹¹ ... above it columns ¹² ... purple, red. And
the tops ¹³⁻¹⁸ (*barely legible remains*).

Column 11

¹⁻⁹ ... ¹⁰ ... and on the day of the sheaf-waving ¹¹ ... [the first-
fru]its for the corn-offering ¹² ... and on the (?) six days ¹³ ... of
Tabernacles and for the solemn assembly ¹⁴ ... [in]ner ... ¹⁵⁻¹⁶ ...

Column 12

¹⁻⁷ ... ⁸ ... its dimensions (?) ⁹ ... cubit ¹⁰ ... all of it ¹¹ ... all
¹² ... ¹³ and its ho[rns (?) and its cor]ners (?) ... to it (?) ... ¹⁴⁻¹⁷
(*very slight traces of letters*)

Column 13

See Yadin III, plate 6*

[1] so that ... [2] [and (?)] ten ... [3] [you shall] make ... [4] and door[s] ...
[5] ... one ... [6] overlaid (?) ... [7] for it a door ... [8] ... [9] ... [10] of the
blood for the people (?) ... [11] without blemish, t[wo] ... [12] fine
flour, mixed ... [12a] and its drink-offering ... [13] for YHWH. ... [14] of
the burnt-[offering] ... [15] like the cereal-of[fering of the] morning ...
[16] You shall not ... [17] And on the S[abbath (?)] days you shall offer
two ...

Column 14

[1] ... [2] [and as a cereal-of]fering fine flour, mix[ed] ... [3] [hal]f of a
hin ... [4] ... with a third [of a *hin*] ... [5] ... tenth as a cereal-
[offering] ... [6] ... for the one (?) lamb ... [as an odour] [7] soothing
to YHWH at the be[ginnings (?) of your months (?)] ... [8] for (?) the
months of the year ... [9] and on the first (?) of the [first] month
... [10] of the year. [You shall abstain] from carrying out any
w[ork] ... [11] separately it shall be brought to at[one for] ... [12] one
ram, lambs of [one year] ... [13] ... [14] [°half (?) of a *hin*] ... as a
drink-offering ... [15] [a tenth of fine flour as a cereal-offering] ...
[16] [third (?) of a *hin* for the one ram°], and for the sheep ... [t]enth
[17] ... cereal-offering mixed with a quarter of a *hin* ... [18] ... one for
the sheep and for the he-[goats] ...

Column 15

Within ° ° the text of Rockefeller Museum fragments 43.976 and 43.978; see
Yadin III, plate 35*

[1] [on ea]ch (?) and every day ... [2] °seven years, and a he-° [goat] ...
[3] [according] to this ordinance. [°And for the consecration a ram for
e° ach day (?)] [3a] [and] baskets of bread for all the ra[ms, one] [4] [for]
each [ram]. And they will divide a[°ll the rams and the baskets over
the sev° en days of the consecration] [5][day] by day according to
[their] division[s °they shall sacrifice to YHWH] [6] as a burnt-
offe° ring from the ram and ... [which on °the] [7] kidneys and [the]
fat [which is on° them] ... [8] the flanks and the rump completely °as
far as the tail-bone and the appendage of the liver.° [9] And its cereal-

offering and its drink-offering according to the pr[escription . . . °the cake] [10] of bread-and-oil and one flat[cake°] . . . [11] with the leg of heave-offering °wh[ich is to the right and those who offer there shall wave°] [12] °the rams and the baskets with bread° as a wa[ve-offering be °fore YHWH. It is a burnt-offering] [13] as a fire-offering a soothing odour° befo[re YHWH] . . . [14] the °burnt-offering in order to undertake it for the se[ven da° ys of the consecration]. [15] °And if the High° Priest st[ands to] . . . [16] . . . °to p[ut o]n the garme° n[ts instead of °his father (?), they sacrifi° ce the young bull(s)], [17] [one] for the whole people (?) and one for the prie[s °ts. And he sacrifices°] [18] [°the one° for the prie °st]s fir° [st] and the elders of the priest[s] lay [their hands] °[on] its he[ad] and after them the H[igh] Priest (?) and all t[he Priests] . . . And the elders of the priests shall take of the blood of the young bull and . . . they shall pour [blood] round about on the f[ou]r corners of the enclosure of the [altar]°

Column 16

[1] . . . [2] . . . [gi]ve of the blood . . . [3] . . . the right and . . . [4] . . . [s]hall he be all his days . . . [5] . . . he [shall not] make himself impure for ho[ly is he] . . . [6] . . . [on the alt]ar and offer up in fire t[he] . . . [7] [the fat wh]ich is on the entrails and . . . [8] [kidn]eys and the fat on the[m] . . . [the] [9] flanks and its cereal-offering and its drin[k-offering] . . . [10] It is [a burnt]-offering, a fire-offering as a soothing odour for [YHWH. (?) And its flesh (?)] [11] and its skin together with the contents of its stomach they shall burn out[side the Holy (?) City] [12] in a place set apart for sin-offerings; there they shall bu[rn it (?)] [13] with all its inward parts and they shall burn it there completely apart from its fat; it [is] a sin-[offering.] [14] And then he shall take the second young bull which is (intended) for the people and through it he shall atone [for the whole people (?)] [15] of the community with its blood and with its fat; as he did with the fi[rst] young bull, [so he shall do] [16] with the young bull of the community. And with his finger he shall put some of its blood on the horns of t[he altar and] [17] he shall sprinkle its blood o[n the fo]ur corners of the enclosure of the altar, and i[ts fat and] [18] its [cereal]-offering and its d[rink-offering] he shall cause to go up in smoke on the altar; [it] is a sin-offering of the community.

Column 17

[1] ... [the pr]iests and give ... [2] ... and they will rejoice because atonement has been made for them ... [3] ... this day will be (?) for them ... [4] ... [in all] their habitations and they will rejoice and ... [5] ... [6] ... [on the fou]rteenth of the first month ... [7] ... and they shall sacrifice before the evening offering (*i.e. the Tamid*) and they shall sacrifice ... [8] [from t]went[y ye]ars and over they shall do it and they shall [eat it during the night (?)] [9] in the courtyard[s of the san]ctuary and each one shall set off early to [his] ten[t]. [10] And on the fifteenth of this month there shall be a h[oly] convocation; [11] you shall abstain [from car]rying out [any] work on it—the Feast of Mazzoth (= *Unleavened Bread*)—for seven days [12] [for] YHWH. And you shall offer on each single day of th[ese] seven days [13] a burnt-offering for YHWH: two young bulls and a ram and sev[en] year-old lambs [14] [wi]thout blemish and one he-goat for the sin-offering as well as its cereal-offering and its drink-offering [15] [according to the prescrip]tion for the young bulls and for the ram and f[or the lam]bs and for the goat. And on the seventh day [16] [there will be a holy convocation for YH]WH; you shall not undertake any task of work on it.

Column 18

See Yadin III, plate 10*

[1] ... [2] ... for this ram ... [3] ... this day ... [4] ... he-g[oat] for the sin-offering ... [5] ... [its cereal-offering and] its [drink]-offering according to prescription, a tenth of fine flour [6] ... wine for the drink-offering, a quarter of a *hin* [7] ... the community from all guilt ... [8] ... [sta]tutes fo[r ever] this will be for ... [9] ... and afterwards they shall offer up the ram as a burnt-offering, one ... [10] ... on the day of sheaf-waving. And cou[nt] [11] [for yourself (*-selves?*) seven] complete [sab]baths from the day of your [off]ering the sheaf [12] ... [cou]nt, until the day following the seventh sabbath count [13] [fifty] days and offer a new cereal-offering to YHWH from your habitations [14] ... new leavened (bread) as first-fruits for YHWH, two (loaves) of wheat bread [15] ... tenths of fine flour will be one offered loaf [16] ... according to the tribes of Israel. And they shall offer

Column 19

Within ° ° the text of Rockefeller Museum fragments 44.008 and 43.975

[1] ... [2] ... the bur[nt-offering (?)] ... [3] ... [t]wel[ve] ... [4] ...
according to the prescription. And wav[e (?)] ... [5] ... [the] first-
fruits °(shall) be[long to] the priests [and they shall eat them] [6] [in
the inner cour° tyard] ... bread of the first-fruits and after ... [7] ...
[°new bread, te]nder ears° and ripe ears (of corn) ... [8] ... [as a
statute for ev]er for their generations. From any under °taking of
wo[rk ab° stain] [9] [on it, for] it is [the Feast of We]eks and the
Festival of the First-fruits as a remembrance for ev[er] [10] ...
[11] [And coun]t for yourselves from the day when you brought the
new cereal-offering for YHW[H,] [12] [the bre °ad] of the first-fruits,
seven we° eks (?), seven complete sabbaths [13] [it will be unti]l the
day after the °seventh° Sabbath; °count fifty° days, [14] [and then
brin]g new wine for the drink-offering, four *hins* from all the tribes
°of Israel, [15] [a third] of a *hin* for° each tribe. And they shall offer
{this} wine on this day [16] [°for YHWH tw]elve rams all° the leaders of
the thousands of Israel.

Continuation of the text between columns 19–20 according to Rockefeller
Museum fragment 43.975, lines [e-k]

[e] ... [the ra]ms and their cereal-offering according to prescription,
two [f] ... [hi]*ns* of oil for each ram for this drink-offering [g] ...
[lamb]s, one year old, seven and a goat [h] ... [c]ommunity. [i] ...
[their cereal-offering] and their drink-offering according to the
prescription for the young bulls and for the rams. X (*scribal mark*)
[j] ... for the quarter of the day they shall offer [k] ... and the drink-
offering, and they shall offer

Column 20

Within ° ° the text of Rockefeller Museum fragments 43.975 and 43.978; see
Yadin III, plates 11* and 36*

[1] ... °and the drink-offering, and they shall offer° ... [2] ... [(one)-
°year-old, fou]r° teen ... [3] ... [°after the burnt-offer]ing they shall
prepare them for° ... [4] ... their fat they shall °cause to rise in smoke

on the al[tar°] ... ⁵ ... and all fa[t] which is on the e[n °trails and the°] ... (?) ⁶ ... [and the appendage of the liver with] the kidneys he shall remove and the fat [which] ... ⁷ ... [t]he ru °mp as far as the° tail bone. And they shall of[fer up in smoke] ⁸ [everything (?) on the altar] with their cereal-offering °and their drink-offering° as a fire-offering, an odour so[ot]hi[ng before ⁹ YHWH]. ... [and they shall of]fer (?) every cereal-offering with which a drink-offering is connected, ... ¹⁰ [and ev °ery cereal-offering° , w]hich is connected with incense or is dry, from which they shall take a handful as its ¹¹ [memorial portio]n and cause it to rise in smoke on the altar; and the remainder of it they shall eat in the i[nner (?)] ¹² court[yard, as unleavened (bread)] the priests shall e[a]t it. It shall not be eaten as leavened (bread). On the same day it shall be ea[ten ¹³ before the setting] of the sun. And on all your offerings put salt. And °the covenant of salt° shall not ce °[a]se ¹⁴ for ever° (*cf. Num. 18.19*). And they shall raise up for YHWH a heave-offering ¹⁵ [°from the ra]ms and from the lambs the right hindleg° and the breast and the ¹⁶ [chops and the stomach] °and the upper foreleg as far as the shoulder bone° , and they shall wave them as a wave-offering

Column 21

Continuation of the text between columns 20 and 21 according to Rockefeller Museum fragment 43.975, lines ᵃ⁻ᵉ

ᵃ ... [shall b]e the shoulder of the heave-offering and the breast ᵇ ... and the cheeks and the stomachs as portions ᶜ ... And the shoulder which is left over from the upper foreleg ᵈ ... as a statute for ever for them and their descendants ᵉ ... [comma]nders of the thousands [from t]he rams and from

Column 21

Within ° ° the text of Rockefeller Museum fragment 43.975; see Yadin III, plates 11* and 37*

¹ ... [on °e ram, one lamb, and for each tribe°] ² ... one for all trib[es (*or: for each tribe ?*)] ... [of the twe °lve tribes of Israel and they shall eat it°] ... ³ ... [in the oute]r [court] before YHWH ... ⁴ ... °[the priests shall drink] first° and the Levites [after them] ...

⁵ ... [al]l lead °ers of the divisions at fir[st X(*scribal mark*)°] ...
⁶ ... and after them the whole people both grea[t] an °d [small and
they shall begin ⁷ to drink new wine]° ... [but they shall not eat] any
[un]ripe grap[es] from the vine ... ⁸ On thi °s° day °they shall make
atonement for the] wine and° the Israelites °shall rejoice° be[fore
YH]WH ⁹ ... [a statute for] ever for their generation °s in all their
habitations and they shall rejoice° on [this] d[ay] ¹⁰ ... [for they
shall begin] to offer as a drink-offering an intoxicating drink, new
wine on the altar of YHWH °year by yea[r] ... ° ¹¹ ... ¹² [And you
shall] cou[nt (?) for yoursel]ves from th °is [day] seven weeks, seve° n
times, forty- ¹³ nine days, there shall be seven complete sabbaths,
until the day °after the ¹⁴ the seventh sabbath° you shall count fifty
days, and then offer new oil from the habitations ¹⁵ [of the tribes of
Is °rae]l, half a *hin*° for each tribe, new oil of crushed olives
¹⁶ ... fresh oil on the altar of the burnt- °offering as first-fruits°
before YHWH

Column 22

Within ° ° the text of Rockefeller Museum fragments 43.976 and 42.178; see
Yadin III, plates 37* and 12*

°a ... b ... with it for the whole community before °[YHWH] ... with
this oil, half of a *hin* ... [according to the prescrip]tion; it is a burnt-
offering, as a fire-offering, an odour ^e [soothing for YHWH] ... they
shall burn this oil ¹ [in the lamps°] ... ² ... °commanders of the
thous[ands with the lead° ers] ... ³ ... o[ne-year-old] lam[bs],
fourt[ee °n, with their cereal-offering and their drink-offering°] ...
⁴ ... for the rams. And the sons of Levi shall slaughter t[he] ... ⁵ ...
°[the priests, the sons] of Aa° ron their blood ... ⁶ ... and their fat
they shall cause to rise in smoke on the altar of the [burnt-offering] ...
⁷ [and their cereal-offering] and their drink-offering they shall cause
to rise in smoke over the piece[s] of fat, [an odour] ⁸ soothing (?) [for
Y]HWH. And they shall raise as a heave-offering from ... ⁹ the right
hindleg and the breast °of the wave-offering and, as° the choice part,
[the upper foreleg and] the (?) ¹⁰ cheeks and the stomach. It shall
belong to the priests as a portion °according to their prescription, and
to the Levites° ... ¹¹ The other shoulder they shall bring out to the
Israelites. And the sons °of Israel° shall give °to the priests° ¹² one
ram (and) one lamb, and to the Levites one ram (and) one lamb, and

(thus) for each and every [13] °tribe one ram (and) one la° mb, and they shall eat them on the same day in the outer court [14] before YHWH, as statutes for °ever for their generations° year by year. Afterwards, [15] they shall eat and anoint themselves from the new oil and from the olives, °for on this day their sins are atoned for° [16] [with respect to all the fresh] oil of the land before YHWH, once a year, and they shall rejoice

Column 23

Within ° ° the text of Rockefeller Museum fragment 42.178 line g; see Yadin III, plate 37*

[g] [°all the sons] of Israel in a° [ll] ... (*four lines lost*) [1] ... [2] ... which ... [3] ... as a burnt-offering for YH[WH] ... [4] ... tw[o he-g]oats ... [5] ... their [cereal-offering] and their drink-offering according to the p[rescription] ... [6] ... one young bull, one ram, [one] lam[b] ... [7] ... [tr]ibe by tribe [the tw]elve sons of Jac[ob ... [8] ... on the altar (?) after the burnt-offering of the T[amid] ... [9] ... the Hi[gh] Priest ... [10] first and after it he shall cause to rise in smoke the burnt-offering of the tribe of Judah and a[s] [11] he causes (it) to rise in smoke they shall slaughter before him the he-goat first and he shall [bring?] [12] its blood to the altar with a sprinkling bowl, and he shall put some of its blood with his finger on the four horns of the alt[ar] [13] of the burnt-offering and on the four corners of the enclosure of the altar and (then) he shall sprinkle its blood on the founda[tion] [14] of the enclosure of the altar round about. And he shall cause its fat to rise in smoke on the altar: the fat which covers the [15] entrails, and which is on the entrails, and the appendage of the liver with the kidneys [16] he shall remove, and the fat which is on them and which is on the flanks he shall cause to rise in smoke, [17] all of it on the altar, with its cereal-offering and its drink-offering, as fire-offerings, a soothing odour for YHWH. And ...

Column 24

[1] ... the he[ad (?)] ... [2] ... and the ... [3] ... [t]he breast with ... [4] ... the lower legs and ... [5] ... [cereal-offeri]ng of its oil and the drink-offering [of its wine (?)] ... [6] ... the flesh for an odour [soothing] ... [7] ... young bull and for each and every ram and [for] ... [8] and its (*i.e. of the burnt-offering*) (sacrificial) parts (?) shall

b[e] (set) apart [and] its [cereal-offering] and its drink-offering on it, a statute [for] ever [9] for their generations before YHWH. [10] And after this burnt-offering he shall make the burnt-offering of the tribe of Judah by itself; a[s] [11] he did with the burnt-offering of the Levites so shall he do with the burnt-offering of the sons of Judah after the [Levites (?)]. [12] And on the second day he shall first make the burnt-offering of Benjamin and after [it] [13] he shall make the burnt-offering of the sons of J{eh}oseph together, Ephraim and Manasseh. And on the third day he shall make [14] the burnt-offering of Reuben by itself and the burnt-offering of Simeon by itself. And on the fourth day [15] he shall make the burnt-offering of Issachar by itself and the burnt-offering of Zebulun by itself. And on the fifth day [16] he shall make the burnt-offering of Gad by itself and the burnt-offering of Asher by itself. And on the sixth day

Column 25

See Yadin III, plate 13*

[1] ... he shall offer ... [2] ... [3] ... festal tumult ... [4] ... [befo]re YHWH ... [5] ... year ... [6] ... their cereal-offering and their drink-offering (?) according to t[heir] prescription ... [7] ... of the *Tamid* offering ... after ... [8] [and] this at the thi[rd] (hour) of the day, [stat]utes for ever for yo[ur] generations ... [9] [you shall] rejoice on this day and abstain from undertaking any wo[rk]: it is a day of rest [10] [for] you this day. And on the tenth of this month is [11] the Day of Atonement. And on it you shall humble your souls (*i.e. fast*), for every soul which does not [12] humble itself on this very day shall be rooted out from its people. And on it you shall offer as a burnt-offering [13] for YHWH one young bull, one ram, seven year-old lambs (*erasure*), one he-[14] goat for the sin-offering—apart from the sin-offering of the atonement—and their cereal-offering, and their drink-offering [15] according to their prescription for the young bull, for the ram, for the lambs and for the goat. And for the sin-offering of the atonement you shall offer [16] two rams as a burnt-offering. The High Priest shall offer one for himself and for his father's house

Column 26

[1-4] (*barely legible remains of letters*) [5] [he shall] slaughter the goat

which . . . [6] its blood with the gold sprinkling bowl which is in . . . [7] of the young bull which he has and atones through it for all the peo[ple of t]he community. And its fat and the cereal-offering [8] of its drink-offering he shall cause to rise in smoke on the altar of the burnt-offerings and its flesh and its skin and the contents of its stomach [9] they shall burn with the young bull. This is the sin-offering of the community and he atones through it for all the people of the community [10] so that they will be forgiven. Then he washes the blood of the sin-offering from his hands and his feet and comes to [11] the (still) living goat and confesses over its head all the iniquities of the Israelites with [12] all their guilt together with all their sin, and he lays them on the head of the goat. Then they send (it) (*or: he sends it*) [13] to Azazel into the desert with a man who is waiting ready. Thus the goat bears all the iniquities

Column 27

[1] . . . [2] for {a[ll]} the sons of Israel, so that [they] will be forgiven . . . [3] Afterwards he shall prep[are] the young bull and t[he ram] and t[he] . . . [4] on the altar for burnt-offerings and the [burnt]-offering shall create favour for the Israelites; a sta[tute] for ev[e]r [5] for their generations. [On]ce a year for them this day shall be as a remembrance, [6] and on it they shall do no work, for it shall be a day of rest [for t]hem and any man [7] who undertakes work on it or who does not humble himself (*i.e. fast*) on it will be rooted out from [8] your people. This day shall be a day of rest and a holy convocation for you [9] and you shall sanctify it as a remembrance in all your habitations and do no [10] work. And on the [fi]fteenth day of this month

Column 28

[1] . . . [2] the altar (?) as a fire-offering, an o[dour soothing] . . . [on the] [3] second [day], twelve young bulls, . . . [4] -teen and one he-goat . . . [5] according to their prescription for young bulls and for ra[ms] and for lambs and for the goat as a fire-offering, [6] it is a soothing odour for YHWH. [And] on the third day [7] twelve [youn]g bulls, two rams, [fo]urteen lambs [8] and one he-goat for the sin-offering and their cereal-offering and their drink-offering (!) according to the prescri[p-tion] for young bulls (?), [9] for rams and for lambs and for the goat. And on the f[our]teenth day [10] te[n] young bulls, two rams, fourteen

(one)-year-old lambs [11] and one he-goat for the sin-offering and their cereal-offering and their drink-offering for young bulls

Column 29

Difficult to read; see Yadin III, plates 14* and 15*

[1] and a drink-offering (?) . . . [2] these . . . [3] for a burnt-offering . . . for . . . [4] my [n]ame on it . . . according to the ruling of this prescription (?) [5] as a regular offering by the Israelites apart from their freewill offerings (?) for all . . . [6] for all their drink-offerings [and for al]l their . . . , which they bring to me for favour for t[hem] . . . [7] . . . [and I] shall be for them eternally . . . [8] with them for ever and eternally. And I shall sanctify my [sanc]tuary with my glory for I shall cause [9] my glory to dwell upon it until (?) the day of blessing (?) on which I shall create (anew) my san[ctuary (?)] [10] to prepare it for myself for all [t]ime according to the covenant which I made with Jacob at Bethel

Columm 30

Fragmentary and extremely difficult to read because it is overlaid with the impression of the text from column 29. Partially preserved in reverse image on the back of column 31. See Yadin III, plate 15*

[1] . . . I shall sanctify [2] . . . [3] . . . to make. And ma[ke] [4] . . . to the steps (?) . . . house which you shall build [5] . . . the steps to the north (of) the Temp[le] (as) a square construction, [6] . . . twenty cubits for (each of) its four (outside) corners at a dis[tan]ce from the wall [7] [of the] Temple seven cubits to the north-west of it. And you shall make the thickness of its wall four [8] cubits . . . Temple and its inner dimension from (inner) corner to (inner) corner [9] twelve cubits (?) . . . square, its width is four [10] cubits (?) in [all] its directions and the width of the staircase leads up four steps . . .

Column 31

See Yadin III, plate 16*

[1] . . . [2] . . . the gate [3] . . . [4] . . . the second priest [5] . . . [6] And on the upper storey of the ho[use (of the stairway)] . . . [make a (?) ga]te (?)

open to the roof of the Temple ... [7] this [g]ate to the op[ening] ... , through which one can enter the upper storey of the Temple. [8] [The whole] of this stairway building over[lay] with gold, its walls and its gates and its roof on the inside [9] [and on] the outside, and its pillar and its steps you shall mak[e] according to all that I tell you. [10] [And ma]ke a housing for the laver to the south-[east], square, on all its s[id]es twenty-one [11] [cubits] ... fifty cubits and the width of the wall (is) three cubits. And (the) height [12] twenty cubits ... make gates for it (*i.e. the housing*) from ... the east (?) and from the north [13] and from the west; and the width of the gates shall be four cubits and their height (?) seven (?)

Column 32

Fragmentary and very difficult to read. Partially preserved in reverse image on the back of column 33; the end of lines 4-5 is an impression from column 31. See Yadin III, plate 17*

[1] ... three cub[its] ... [2-5] (*barely legible remains of letters*) [6] ... their guilt to atone for the peop[le] and when [they ?] go up [7] ... to cause their cerea[l-off]ering to rise in smoke on the altar [8] of the burnt-[offering] ... in the wall of the housing, [9] this ... and one cubit and its height ... [10] from the ground four cubits overlaid with gold that they set ... on them (?) [11] their (?) garments when they come in them above ... [12] [when] they come to serve in the sanctuary. And you shall make (?) a channel around the laver, along its housing (?) and the channel [13] shall run [from the housing] of the laver and a shaft which leads down [and] ... into the earth so that [14] the water will run out and flow down to it and disappear into the earth. But no[15] one shall touch it, because the blood of the burnt-offering is mixed in with it.

Column 33

Partially preserved in reverse image on the back of col. 34. See Yadin III, plates 18*-19*

[1] ... [pries]ts come ... [2] ... And at the time wh[en] ... [3] ... [4] ... [the garments (which are on?)] them and se[t (?)] ... [5] ... [6] ... to the basin and go out ... [7] ... sanctify ... holy garments ... [8] [And you] shall make a house to the east of the housing of the [la]ver with

the dimensions [of the hous]ing of the laver [9] [and the dis]tance of its wall from the w[al]l of that (house) shall be seven cubits and its [who]le construction (?) and its timb[erwork like the house of the] laver (?). [10] [And] it shall have two gates, to the north and to the south, the one opposite the [other], having the dimensions of the gate[s] of the housing [11] of the laver. And this entire house, all of it, shall be provided with blind window recesses (?) (on the surface of) its wall(s), [12] two cubits (deep), their width two cubits and their (?) height four [cub]its, [13] provided with doors, as depositories for the altar vessels, for the sprinkling bowls and for the cups and for the fire holders [14] and for the silver bowls (?) in which they bring the entrails and the [15] feet (?) onto th[e a]ltar. And when they have finished causing to rise in smoke (?)

Column 34

Very difficult to read; partially preserved in reverse image on the back of column 35. See Yadin III, plates 20* and 21*

[1] ... on a tablet of bro[nze] ... [2] ... and between the column (and) t[he] ... [3] ... which between the columns ... [4] ... between (?) the whe[els] ... [5] ... they lock (?) the wheels ... [6] and bind the heads (horns?) of the young bulls (?) into the rings ... [r]ings, [7] afterwards they shall slaughter them (?). And they shall collect [their blood] in sprinkling bowls [8] and they shall sprinkle it on the base (?) of the altar round about. Then they shall unlock (?) [9] the wheels and pull the skins of the young bulls from their flesh and cut [10] them up into their parts and salt the parts with salt (?) and wash the [11] entrails and the lower legs and salt them with salt (?) and cause them to rise in smoke over [12] the fire which is on the altar, young bull by young bull, with its parts and the cereal-offering of its fine flour upon it, [13] and the wine of its drink-offering with it, and with its oil upon it. And the priests, the sons of Aaron, shall cause everything to rise in smoke [14] on the altar as a fire-offering, a soothing odour before YHWH. [15] And you shall make chains that shall hang down from the framework of the twelve columns

Column 35

Difficult to read; at times easier to read as reverse image on the back of column 36. See Yadin III, plates 22* and 23*

[1] ... holy ... [2] ... every one who ... [3] ... every one (?) who not ...
[4] ... ou[t of i]t ... [5] ... And each ... who comes [6] ... and he has
not put on (?) ... has 'filled [7] his hands' (*i.e. has been consecrated*),
they shall also be killed (?), and they shall not dese[crate the
sanct]uary for their God to take [8] upon themselves the guilt of sin
(which leads) to death and sanctify the surroundings of the altar and
of the Temple and of the laver [9] and of the ... so that they will be
most holy for ever and eternally. [10] And you shall make a place to the
west of the Temple round about as a columned porch (*i.e. peristyle*)
of (free-)standing columns [11] for the sin-offering and for the guilt-
offering, separated from one another (on one side) for the sin-offering
of the priests and for the goats, [12] and (on the other side) for the sin-
offering of the people and for their guilt-offering. Under no circumstances shall they be confused with [13] one another; therefore their
places shall be kept apart from one another so that [14] the priests shall
[not] err with regard to all the sin-offering of the people and with
regard to all [the] rams [of the] guilt-offerings (*or with Yadin:* ... '*of
the people and in all of them lies guilt*') to take upon themselves [15] the
guilt of sin. And (as for) the birds upon the altar: he shall prepare the
turtle doves

Column 36

See Yadin III, plate 24*

[1-3] (*barely legible remains of letters*) [4] ... of the ga[te] ... the gate ...
[forty (?) [5] cubits], in each direction ... seven (?) ... [6] [and its
heig]ht [forty]-five cubits (?) ... roo[f] ... [twenty]-[7] six cubits [from]
(one inner) corner to (the other inner) corner ... and the g[at]es.
(through) which they enter [8] and (through) which they g[o o]ut, the
[clear] width of the gate is four[tee]n cubits and their (?) height
[9] [twenty]-eight cubits from the threshold to the lintel, and the
height [10] [of the timberwork] from the lintel is fourteen cu[bi]ts; and
it shall be furnished (?) with panelling [11] of cedar wood, [over]laid
[with] pure gold and its doors will be overlaid with fine gold. [12] And
from the (outer) corner of the gate as far as the second (inner) corner
of the court shall be a hundred and [13] twenty cubits. And the same
shall be the mea{su}rements of all th[es]e gates [w]hich [14] belong to
the inner [c]ourt. And the gateways shall project into the court

Column 37

See Yadin III, plate 25*. Within ° ° the text of Rockefeller Museum fragment
43.978, Yadin III, plate 38*

1-3 . . . 4 the inner (?) [court] to the enclosure of the [alta]r . . . 5 [the
sh]*elamim*-sacrifices of the Israelites . . . 6 . . . of the lower (?) columned
portico . . . 7 . . . on both [sides (?) of the gate (?)]. 8 And you shall
m[ak]e in the [court in]side se[at]s (?) for the [priests (?) and tables]
9 in front of the seats in the inner columned portico on the wall of the
outer court, 10 places prepared for (the) priests [for their sacrifices (?)
and for the °first-fruits and for the tithes°] 11 and for their *shelamim*-
sacrifices which . . . there shall not be m[ix °ed] the *shelamim*-12
sacrifices of the sons of Isr° ael with the sacrifices of the [pri]ests.
13 And in the four (inner) corners of the court [you] shall [ma]ke for
them a p °lace [for herds], 14 where they° shall cook their sacrifices
[and] the sin-offerings

Column 38

Very badly preserved; see Yadin III, plate 26*. Within ° ° the text of
Rockefeller Museum fragment 43.366, Yadin III, plate 38*

1 . . . [they shal]l eat . . . 2 . . . 3 . . . they shall eat . . . 4 . . . °to corn
and to wine° and to . . . 5 . . . °Israelites. And [on the day of the first-
fruits° (?)] . . . 6 . . . by the wes[t] gate . . . °pomegranates° . . . 7 . . .
wood that comes to . . . [°cereal-offering of the sacrifice], 8 on
which° incense comes and . . . offering for °jealousy. 9 And to the
right of this gate° every cereal-offering . . . sin-offering which 10 . . .
there °they shall eat the produce° . . . birds and for doves and turtle
doves . . . 11 (*blank? erased?*) 12 And you shall make a second [c]ourt
around the inner court, width (*i.e. depth*) one hundred cubits 13 °and
the length towards° the east four hundred and eighty cubits and the
same (?) is the width and len °gth in all 14 its directions° , to the
south and to the west and to the north. And the thickness of the wal[l
is fo]ur cubits and the height twenty 15 eight cubits. And recesses
shall be made in the wall on the outside, and °between the individual
recesses three cubits and a half°

Column 39

Only the lower portion has been preserved to any extent; see Yadin III, plate 27*

1-2 ... 3 ... doors ... 4 ... this court ... 5 ... fou[rth (?)] generation ... 6 ... before all ... 7 Israel ... a woman or a child until the
day 8 when it fulfils the prescription ... as the [sum of] his redem[p-
tion] for YHWH the half-shekel ... 9 as a remembrance ... 10 And
when [they take the half-shekel from him] ... Afterwards they may
enter (?) from 11 twe[nty (years)] ... And the na[mes of the ga]tes of
this [co]urt according to the [names (?)] 12 of the sons [of Israe]l:
Simeon, Levi and Judah in the east, [and Re]uben, Joseph and
Benjamin in the 13 south; Issachar, Zebulun and Gad in the west;
Dan, Naphtali and Asher in the north. And from gate to gate 14 [the]
measurement is: from the (outer) corner in the north-east to the gate
of Simeon ninety-nine cubits, and the gate (itself) 15 twenty-eight
cubits and from this gate {of Simeon} to the gate ... of Levi ninety-
nine 16 cubits, and the gate (itself) twenty-eight cubits. And from the
gate of L[evi to the gate of J]udah

Column 40

Difficult to read; see Yadin III, plate 28*

1 ... to put on the ga[rments (?)] ... 2 ... to be ... 3 ... sons of
Israel and not ... 4 ... 5 ... And you shall make a t[hird] court ...
6 ... for their daughters and for the proselytes who are bor[n] ...
7 ... [the ar]ea around the middle court ... 8 in length (about?) one
thousand and si[x hundred] cubits from (outer) corner (building) to
(outer) corner (building) on each side according to this measurement,
9 to the east (?) and south (?) and to the west (?) and to the n[ort]h.
And the thickness of the wall is seven cubits and (the) height forty-
10 nine cubits. And recesses shall be pl[ac]ed between its gatehouses,
on the outside, from the foundation 11 as far as its crowns (?). Three
(?) (are) [its] gates in the east and three in the south and three 12 in
the west and three to the north, and the width of the gates is fifty
cubits and its height seventy 13 cubits. And between the gates [the
measurement is] three hundred and sixty cubits, from the (outer)
corner (building) to the 14 gate of Simeon three hundred and sixty

cubits, and from the gate of Simeon to the gate of Levi [15] according to this measurement, and from the ga[te] of Levi to the gate of Judah according to this measurement, three hundred and

Column 41

From line 4 the text is completed from Rockefeller Museum fragment 43.366; see Yadin III, plates 29* and 38*

[01] [sixty cubits (*etc.*)] ... [1] ... [g]ate [2] ... this [(outer) corner] [3] to the g[ate of Issachar ... cubits and from the gate [4] of Issachar ... three hundred and [sixty] cubits [5] and from the gate of Zeb[ulun to the gate of Gad] three hundred [and six]ty [6] cubits and from the g[ate of Gad to the (outer) corner ... three hundred [7] and sixty cubits. ... [And] from this (outer) corner to the [8] gate of Dan three hundred and sixty cubits, and the same from the gate of Dan to the [9] gate of Naphtali, three hundred and sixty cubits, and from the gate of Naphtali [10] to the gate of Asher three hundred and sixty cubits, and from the gate [11] of Asher to the (outer) corner of the east three hundred and sixty cubits. [12] And the gateways shall project from the wall of the court seven cubits to the outside [13] and on the inside they shall project thirty-six cubits from the wall of the court. [14] And the width of the gate openings shall be fourteen cubits and their height [15] is twenty-eight cubits to the lintel. And (they shall be) furnished [16] with jambs of cedar wood and overlaid with gold, and their doors overlaid [17] with pure gold. And between the gates make cells on the inside

Column 42

Text of lines 8*-11* from Rockefeller Museum fragment 43.366; see Yadin III, plate 38* and also II, 122. For the text of lines 1ff. see Yadin III, plate 29*, bottom

[8*] The width of the back room amounts to ten cubits, its length twenty cubits, its height fou[rteen cubits] ... [9*] cedar wood and the thickness of the wall is two cubits. And outside it are the cells ... [10*] twenty cubits, and the wall two cubits. The width ... [11*] cedar wood. And the door opening is three cubits wide ... [1] ... [2] ... the lintel ... [3] ... for all the cells and their chambers [4] ... [wid]th ten cubits and between gate [5] and gate ... [eigh]teen cells

and their chambers [6] eigh[teen] . . . [7] And make a staircase on the walls of the gates in the [8] portico, (by which) they shall go up (on) steps leading up and round into the second and third portico [9] and onto the roof. And the cells and their chambers and their porticos are built as the bottom, [10] second, and third stories, following the measurements of the bottom one. And on the roof over the third (storey) [11] make columns, furnished with beams from column to column, [12] as a place for the tabernacles, eight cubits high. And the tabernacles shall be [13] made on them every year at the Feast of Tabernacles for the elders [14] of the community, for the leaders, for the heads of the houses of the fathers of the Israelites [15] and for the commanders of the thousands and for the commanders of the hundreds, so that they will go up [16] and sit there during the offering of the festal offering which [17] (is specified) for the Feast of Tabernacles year by year. Between one gate and another they shall

Column 43

[1] . . . [2] . . . on the days of the sabbaths and on the day[s] . . . [3] . . . and on the days of the first-fruits for corn, for w[ine and for oil] [4] [and on the festival of the] wood-[offering]. On these days it shall be eaten, but they shall not leave to lie . . . [5] [from one year] to another year, for so shall they eat it: [6] [from the] festival of the first-fruits of wheat grain they shall eat the grain [7] until the second year, until the festival of the first-fruits; and the wine from the appointed festival [8] of the (new) wine until the second year, until the day of the appointed festival [9] of the (new) wine and the fresh oil from the day of its appointed festival until the second year, [10] until the appointed festival of the day of offering new oil on the altar, and everything [11] which is left over beyond its appointed festival shall cease to be holy. It is to be burned in fire; it is no longer permitted to be eaten, [12] for it has ceased to be holy. And those who live further from the sanctuary than a distance of three [13] days shall bring everything that they can bring and if they are unable [14] to carry it they shall sell it for money and bring the money, and with it they shall (then) buy grain [15] and wine and oil and cattle and sheep and eat it at the time of their appointed festivals. But they shall not [16] eat from it on work-days with the distress of their labour, for it is holy; [17] and on the holy days it shall be eaten but it shall not be eaten on work-days

Column 44

[1] ... [l]iving ... [2] ... who within the city ... [3] ... And you shall divide th[e] ... [From the gate [4] of Simeon] to the gate of Judah shall belong to the priests ... [5] and [every]thing to the right of the gate of Levi and to the left of it. To the sons of Aaron, your brothers, al[lot] [6] one hundred and eight cells and their chambers and their tabernacles [7] which are on the roof. And to the sons of Judah (allot) from the gate of Judah to [8] the (outer) corner (building) fifty-four cells and their chambers and the tabernacle [9] which is above them. And to the sons of Simeon (allot) from the gate of Simeon to the second (outer) corner (building) [10] their cells and their chambers and their tabernacle(s). And to the sons of Reuben (allot) [11] from the (inner) corner which is with the sons of Judah to the gate of Reuben [12] fifty-two cells and their chambers and their tabernacle(s). And from the gate [13] of Reuben to the gate of Joseph (allot) to the sons of Joseph, to Ephraim and to Manasseh. [14] And from the gate of Joseph to the gate of Benjamin (allot) to the sons of Kahath, fr[om] the Levites. [15] And from the gate of Benjamin to the western (outer) corner (building) (allot) to the sons of Benjamin. And from this [16] (outer) corner (building) to the gate of Issachar (allot) to the sons of Issachar; and from the gate

Column 45

[01-04] [of Issachar] ...

[1] and from ... [2] sevent[y] ... [3] and there ... he sha[l]l enter to the left ... [4] the first shall go out from [the right (?)]; but they [shall not] become mixed up with one another with (their) vessels ... [5] a priestly course on duty at their place, mounting guard; on the eighth day, as one [enters] the other departs, then they clean the [6] cells, one after the other [at the ti]me when the first goes out; there cannot be [7] any mixing there. And if o[ne] has an emission of a semen in the night, then he may not enter [8] the whole sanctuary until he has [comp]leted three days. He shall wash his clothes and bathe [9] on the first day, and on the third day he shall wash his clothes {and bathe}, and after the sun has set, [10] he may come to the sanctuary. But in their sexual impurity they may not come into my sanctuary to make [it] unclean. [11] If a man lies with his wife with emission of semen he may not enter any (part) of the city [12] of the sanctuary, in which I

cause my name to dwell, for three days. No blind people [13] may enter it all their days lest they defile the city in whose midst [14] I dwell, for I, YHWH, dwell amongst the sons of Israel for ever and eternally. [15] And any man who is cleansed of his discharge shall count for himself seven days for his cleansing, and on the seventh [16] day wash his garments and bathe the whole of his body with living water; afterwards he may come to the city [17] of the sanctuary. And none who are unclean (by virtue of contact with) a corpse may enter it before they are cleansed. And no lepers, [18] nor those smitten (with a skin disease), may enter it before they are cleansed. And when he is cleansed he shall offer

Column 46

See Yadin III, plates 30* and 39* (Rockefeller Museum fragment 43.976)

[1] ... [shall n]ot [fly any (?)] [2] unclean [b]ird over [my] san[ctuary] ... roofs of the gate, [which [3] (belong) to the] outer court. And ... [to b]e in my sanctuary for ev[er] [4] and eternally all the days that I [dwe]ll in their midst. [5] And you shall make a terrace round about outside the outer court (with a) width (of) [6] fourteen cubits corresponding to (*or: before*) all the gate openings and you shall make [7] twelve steps for it, so that the Israelites may go up to it [8] to come into my sanctuary. [9] And you shall make an embankment around the sanctuary, one hundred cubits wide, so that it [10] divides the holy sanctuary from the city and they shall not enter unprepared into [11] my sanctuary and they shall not profane it, but shall keep my sanctuary holy and conduct themselves respectfully towards my sanctuary, [12] where I dwell in their midst. [13] And you shall make for them a privy outside the city, to which they may go out, [14] outside, to the north-west of the city, small houses, and furnished with beams and with holes in them [15] through which the excrement may fall down and {not} remain visible, (and) with a minimum distance [16] from the city of three thousand cubits. And you shall make [17] three places to the east of the city, separated from one another to which shall [18] come the lepers and those afflicted with discharge and the people who have emission of semen

Column 47

See Yadin III, plate 39*

[1] ... [2] ... above and not be[low] ... [3] ... clean and ... for ever. But the city [4] [w]hich I consecrate, so that my name and [my (?)] san[ctuary] ... shall be present, is to be holy and clean [5] from everything with which an impurity is connected, and through which they can become unclean. Everything in it shall be [6] clean and everything which enters it shall be clean, wine and oil and all food [7] and all drink shall be clean. No hide of any clean animal which they slaughter [8] in their cities may they bring into it (*i.e. the city of the sanctuary*). In their cities they shall carry out [9] their work with them (*i.e. the hides*) according to all their needs, but to the city of my sanctuary they may not bring [them], [10] for as their flesh, so also shall their purity be, and they shall not pollute the city in [11] the midst of which I cause my name and my sanctuary to be present. Rather with the hides (of the animals) which they slaughter [12] in the sanctuary, with them they shall bring their wine and their oil and all [13] their food to the city of my holiness, but they shall not make my sanctuary impure with the hides of their profane [14] slaughterings which they make in their land. You shall not consider any [15] of your cities as (equally) pure as my city, for according to the purity of the flesh so also shall the hides be pure. If [16] you slaughter it in my sanctuary, it is pure according to my sanctuary and if you slaughter it in your cities it is pure [17] according to your cities. Any(thing with the degree of) purity of the sanctuary you shall bring in hides of the sanctuary and not pollute [18] my sanctuary and my city with the skins of your profane slaughterings, for I dwell in it.

Column 48

See Yadin III, plate 32*

[1-2] ... [3] [And of all] the winged (creatures) you may eat: the migratory locust according to [its kinds, and] ... according to its kinds, and the *tettigoniidae* locust [4] according to its kinds, and the *ḥagab* locust according to its kinds. These of the winged creatures you may eat: those which creep on all fours, those which [5] have the thigh above the feet in order to leap up on [from] the ground with them and to fly with their wings. No [6] carcass of winged creatures

and of cattle may you eat: sell it to the stranger, and no abomination
[7] may you eat, for you are a holy people for YHWH, your God. You
are sons [8] for YHWH, your God! You shall not make cuttings in your
skin, and you shall not shave a bald patch over your forehead
[9] because of a dead person, and you shall not make an incision in
your body because of a deceased person, and you shall not make
tattooed writing [10] on yourselves, for you are a holy people for
YHWH your God. So do not defile [11] your land! You shall not do as
the nations do—in every place they (are accustomed) [12] to burying
their dead; even in their houses they bury them—but [13] you shall set
apart places in your land where you shall bury your dead. Among
four [14] cities you shall establish a place for the purpose of burying in
it. And in each and every city you shall establish places for those who
are smitten [15] with leprosy and with sores and with scabs, so that
they shall not enter your cities and defile them. And likewise for
those afflicted with discharge [16] and for the women, when they are in
their menstrual impurity and in their birth impurity, so that they do
not cause impurity in their midst [17] through their sexual impurity.
And the leper on whom there is a chronic leprosis or scab, the priest
shall declare him unclean

Column 49

[1] ... [2] ... them ... [3] ... and with cedar wood and with hyssop and
with ... [4] your cities with the plague of leprosy and (thus) become
unclean. [5] If a man dies in your cities, then the whole of the house in
which the deceased died is unclean [6] for seven days, everything that
is in the house and everything that comes into the house is unclean
[7] for seven days, all food on which {liquid} is poured is unclean, all
drink [8] is unclean. And earthen vessels are unclean and everything
which is in them is, for every clean man, [9] unclean and open (vessels)
are unclean for every man of Israel, (as is) all drink [10] that is in them.
[11] And on the day when they bring out the deceased from it, they
shall clean the house of all [12] tarnishing through oil and wine and
moisture of water. Its floor and its walls and its doors they shall
scrape off [13] and its door locks and its doorposts and its thresholds
and its lintels they shall wash down with water. On the day when
[14] the deceased is brought out from it they shall clean the house and
all its vessels, handmills and mortars [15] and all vessels of wood, iron
and bronze, as with all vessels to which (ritual) purity applies,

16 clothing, sacking and leather shall be washed. And (with regard to) persons: each one who was in the house 17 and each one who came into the house shall bathe in water and wash his clothes on the first day, 18 and on the third day they shall sprinkle cleansing water over them and they shall bathe and wash their garments 19 and the vessels which are in the house. And on the seventh day 20 they shall sprinkle a second time and bathe and wash their garments and their vessels; and they are clean by the evening 21 from the dead person, so that they may touch all their clean things and also (they may touch) any person who has not made himself unclean for

Column 50

See Yadin III, plate 39* (Rockefeller Museum fragment 43.978)

1 ... 2 for the water of puri[fication] ... [m]ixing of the dead [...] 3 were polluted, not ... until they sprinkle the sec[ond (time)] 4 on the seventh day; for they are c[lean by the even]ing when the sun sets. Everyone 5 who in the open field comes into contact with the bones of a dead person, or with one pierced with a sword, 6 or a dead (animal ?), or the blood of a dead person, or a grave, shall cleanse himself as this statute prescribes. 7 And if he does not cleanse himself as prescribed by this ruling, he is unclean: 8 his impurity shall remain clinging to him. Everyone who comes into contact with him shall wash his clothes and bathe, and will be clean 9 by the evening. 10 And if a woman is pregnant and her child dies in her womb, all the days that 11 it is dead within her she is as unclean as a grave. Each house that she enters is unclean, 12 and all its vessels, for seven days, and everyone who comes into contact with it is unclean until the evening. And if he 13 (*i.e. her husband*) comes to her in the house he shall be unclean for seven days. He shall wash his clothes 14 and bathe on the first day {with water}, and on the third day he shall sprinkle (the cleansing water) and wash his clothes and bathe. 15 And on the third day he shall sprinkle a second time and wash his clothes and bathe, and when the sun has gone down 16 he shall be clean. And all vessels and clothes and hides and everything 17 made of goat hair you shall treat as this ruling prescribes, but all vessels 18 of earthenware shall be smashed, for they are unclean and will not become clean 19 ever. 20 Every small living thing of the earth (*or: ground*) you shall consider as unclean, the mole and the mouse and

the lizard according to their kinds, the gecko [21] and the *koah* lizard and the *homet* lizard and the chameleon. Everyone who touches them when they are dead

Column 51

[1] ... unclean [2] ... You shall not pollute yourselves with the[m] ... [when] they are dead, will be unclean [3] u[ntil the] evening. He shall wash his clothes and bathe [in water and by the setting] of the sun he is clean. [4] And everyone who lifts from their bones or from their carcase skin, flesh or claws shall wash his clothes and bathe in water. And after the sun has set he is clean. So warn the [6] the Israelites against all the uncleanness{es}! They shall not defile themselves with the (things) which [7] I tell you on this mountain and not become unclean. For I, YHWH, dwell [8] amongst the Israelites; so make yourselves holy and be holy. And they shall not make themselves into an abomination [9] through anything that I have singled out for uncleanness for them, so that [10] they will be holy. [11] Appoint judges and officers for yourself in all your gates, so that they may judge the people [12] with just judgment, and not exercise personal prejudice in judgment, and not accept bribery, and not [13] pervert justice; for bribery perverts justice, and falsifies the words of justice, and blinds [14] the eyes of the wise, and causes great guilt, and pollutes the house with the guilt [15] of sin. Justice, justice, you shall strive after, so that you may live and come to inherit [16] the land which I give to you as an inheritance for all time. And the man [17] who takes a bribe and perverts justice in judgment shall be killed, and you shall not be afraid [18] of killing him. [19] You shall not behave in your land as the nations behave: in every place they are accustomed to [20] sacrifice and plant for themselves *asherim* and set up for themselves *mazzeboth* [21] and place for themselves stone images, to bow down before them and to build for themselves

Column 52

[1] ... not plant ... [2] ... and do not set up for yourself a *mazz*[ebah] ... [sto]ne [3] [im]age you shall [not] make for yourself in all your land to bow do[wn] before it. And you shall not [4] sacrifice to me an ox or a sheep that is afflicted with any evil blemish, for they are an abomination [5] to me. And you shall not sacrifice to me a cow, a sheep

or a goat when they are heavy with young, for they are an abomination to me. [6] And you shall not slaughter a cow or a sheep with its young on the same day, and you shall not kill the mother [7] with its young. All firstborn which are produced by your herds and flocks, [8] if they are male, you shall dedicate to me. You shall not work with any firstborn bull and you shall not shear the firstborn [9] of your sheep. You shall consume them year by year before me in the place that I shall choose. But if there is [10] a blemish in it, or it is lame, or blind, or if it is afflicted with an evil blemish, you shall not sacrifice it to me; in your gates [11] (*i.e. at home*) you shall eat it, that which is unclean (for the offering) and that which is clean in this way together, like the deer and the gazelle. Only the blood you may not eat: [12] you shall pour it out onto the ground like water and cover it with dust. You shall not muzzle an ox while it is threshing. [13] You shall not plough with an ox and an ass together. You shall not sacrifice clean oxen, sheep or goats [14] in all your gates which are nearer than three days' journey from my sanctuary but in [15] my sanctuary you shall slaughter (it) in order to offer it as a burnt-offering or as a *shelamim*-sacrifice and you shall eat [16] and rejoice before me in the place where I choose to set my name. And all the cattle [17] which are (otherwise) clean (for offering) but which are afflicted with a blemish, you shall eat in your gates, away from my sanctuary [18] (beyond a radius of) thirty *ris* and you shall not slaughter them near my sanctuary, for [it is] the flesh of profane slaughter. [19] You shall not eat the flesh of oxen, sheep and goats in my city, which I sanctify [20] to set my name in it: this shall not come into my sanctuary. They shall slaughter it there [21] and sprinkle its blood on the base of the altar for burnt-offerings and cause its fat to go up in smoke

Column 53

[1] . . . [2] . . . you yourself to eat . . . [3] you shall eat me[at] . . . from your sheep and from your oxen according to my blessing which I bestow [4] upon you. And you shall eat in your gates both that which is clean (for offering) and that which is not clean (for offering) in the same way together, like the deer [5] and the gazelle; only pay firm attention not to eat the blood, which you shall pour on the ground like water and cover [6] with dust, for blood is life, and you may not eat life with flesh—in order that [7] it will go well with you and your sons after you

for ever. So do what is right and good [8] before me, I, (who am) YHWH your God! [9] Only your consecrated gifts and all your vowed (gifts) you shall take, and come to the place where I cause [10] my name to dwell. There you shall sacrifice before me as you have consecrated or vowed with your mouth. [11] For when you make a vow, do not hesitate to fulfil it, for I assuredly demand it from your hand [12] and it shall become a sin (*i.e. liability*) to you. But if you withhold and do not vow, there will be no sin with you. [13] Keep what comes from your lips, as when you vow a freewill offering with your mouth to carry (it) out [14] as you have vowed it. And if a man makes a vow to me, or swears [15] an oath to impose abstinence on himself, he shall not break his words: according to everything that comes out of his mouth [16] he shall act. And if a woman makes an oath to me, or imposes abstinence upon herself [17] in her father's house with an oath in her (premarital) youth, and her father heard her vow or [18] the promise of abstinence which she took upon herself, and kept silent towards her, then [19] all her vows are valid and (also) each of her promises of abstinence, which she took upon herself, is valid. But if [20] her father raises an objection against her on the day when he hears one of her vows and promises of abstinence [21] which she took upon herself, then they are invalid and I will forgive her, for he raised an objection against her.

Column 54

[1] . . . [2] her guilt . . . or any oath of ab[stinence] . . . [3] her husband can declare [it] v[alid and her husband can] abrogate it on the day when he hears it and I will forgive [he]r. [4] Every vow of a widow and a divorcee which she has taken upon herself [5] is valid according to everything that has come from her mouth. All the words, that [6] I command you today you shall observe to fulfil them. You shall not add to them and not [7] take anything away from them. [8] If a prophet arises in your midst or a dream-teller and gives you a sign or [9] a wonder and the sign or the wonder which he had announced to you with these words, [10] 'Let us go and worship other gods whom you do not know', comes true for you, then you shall not [11] listen to the word of this prophet or this dream-teller, for [12] I am testing you to find out if you love YHWH, [13] the God of your fathers, with all your heart and with all your soul. [14] You shall follow after YHWH your God, serve him and fear him and listen to his voice [15] and cling to him! And that prophet or dream-teller shall be killed, for he has

declared disloyalty [16] to YHWH your God, who brought you out of the land of Egypt and redeemed you [17] from the house of slavery, so as to lead you away from the path on which I ordered you to go. Thus you shall eradicate the evil from your midst. [19] And if your brother, the son of your father or the son of your mother, or your son, or your daughter, [20] or the wife of your bosom, or your best friend, misleads you secretly, saying, [21] 'Let us go and worship other gods', whom you do not know, (neither) you

Column 55

See Yadin III, plate 33*

[1] ... [2] If you hear it said about o[ne of the cities which I] give to you to li[ve in] [3] that m[en] have gone out, [worth]less peo[ple] from your midst, and have misled all the [inha]bitants [4] of their city with the words 'Let us go and worship gods, whom you do not know', [5] then enquire and investigate and search thoroughly. And if it proves to be reliably true [6] that this act of abomination has been committed in Israel, then smite all the inhabitants [7] of that city with the edge of the sword; and everything that is in it and [8] all their cattle you shall smite with the edge of the sword. And gather all the booty from it into [9] its main square and burn the city and all its booty as a whole-offering for YHWH, [10] your God. It shall remain for ever as a heap of rubble: it shall not be built up again. And nothing shall remain [11] in your hands of what has been placed under the ban, so that I can desist from the heat of my anger and give you (my) [12] mercy, for I am merciful to you and increase you, as I said to your fathers: [13] 'If you listen to my voice to observe all my commandments which I command you [14] this day to do what is right and good before YHWH your God ... [15] If there shall be in your midst, in one of your gates (*places*) that [16] I give you, a man or a woman who does what is evil in my eyes, [17] to break my covenant, and goes and worships other gods and bows down to them [18] or to the sun or the moon or the whole host of heaven, and they inform you about it, [19] and you have heard this thing, then enquire and investigate thoroughly. If [20] it then proves to be reliably true that this act of abomination has been committed in Israel, then take this man or this woman out and stone them' (*continuation possibly like Dt. 17.5ff.*)

Column 56

[1] ... so enquire ... [2] the matter on account [of which you have come to enquire, and they will ma]ke known to you the judgment [3] and you shall (then) act according to the Torah which they communicate to you and according to the word [4] which they say to you from the book of the Torah and which they reliably make known to you [5] from the place that I shall choose for my name to be present upon it. Be careful to act [6] according to everything they teach you; act according to the judgment which they give you. [7] You shall not deviate from the Torah which they communicate to you (neither) to the right [8] (nor to) the left. And the man who does not wish to hear, and acts presumptuously without [9] listening to the priest who stands there to serve before me, or to [10] the judge, this man shall die. Thus you shall eradicate the evil from Israel and all [11] people shall hear and see it, so that they shall not act presumptuously again in Israel. [12] If you come into the land which I give you, and take possession of it, and settle [13] in it, and then say, 'I shall set over myself a king like all the peoples round about me', [14] then set over yourself a king {whom I shall choose}. From your brothers you shall set a king over yourself, [15] and not set over yourself a stranger who is not your brother. Only he may not [16] keep many horses nor lead the people back to Egypt to war in order [17] to acquire many horses for himself and silver and gold. Surely I have said to you: 'You shall never [18] go back again on this road,' And he shall not acquire many wives, lest they turn his heart away from me. And he shall not acquire silver and gold in excess. [20] And when he sits on the throne of his kingdom, they shall write [21] for him this Torah on a scroll before the priests.

Column 57

[1] And this is the Torah ... priests ... [2] on the day when they install hi[m] as king, ... the Israelites from [3] twenty years old to sixty years old according to their divisions, and he appoints ({they appoint}) [4] at their head commanders of thousands and commanders of hundreds and commanders of fifties [5] and commanders of tens in all their cities. And he shall select for himself a thousand of them [6] from each tribe, so that there are twelve thousand men of war with him [7] who will never leave him alone so that he could be taken by the hand of the nations. And all [8] the selected men whom he has chosen shall be

honest, godfearing, [9] disdaining ill-gotten gain, able-bodied heroes for battle. And they shall remain with him constantly, [10] day and night, to guard him from every offence [11] and from all members of foreign nations, lest he be taken by their hand. Twelve [12] leaders of his people shall be with him, and twelve priests and [13] twelve Levites, to hold session together with him for the administration of justice [14] and for Torah. And he shall not raise his heart above them and he shall do nothing [15] without their advice. He may not take a wife from all [16] the daughters of the nations; rather he shall take for himself a wife from his father's house, [17] from his father's clan. And he may not take any other woman in addition to her, but [18] she alone shall be with him all the days of his life. And if she dies, he shall take [19] for himself another from his father's house, from his clan. He shall not pervert justice [20] and he shall not accept bribery to pervert the righteous administration of justice. And he shall not covet [21] fields, vineyards and any property, houses and anything valuable in Israel so that he steals it

Column 58

[1] ... [2] ... their [m]en. ... [3] And if he {the king} hears concerning any people or nation, that it seeks to steal anything which [4] belongs to Israel, then he shall send (instructions) to the commanders of the thousands and the commanders of the hundreds installed in the cities [5] of Israel, and they shall despatch with him a tenth of the people ({*erasure*}) to go out with him to war against [6] their enemies, and they shall go out with him. But if a large host comes to the land of Israel, then they shall send [7] with him a fifth of the men of war. And if it is a king (with) chariots, horses and many men, [8] then they shall send with him a third of the men of war and the (other) two divisions shall guard [9] their cities and their borders so that no horde will penetrate into their land. [10] And if the war (still) becomes too hard for him, they shall send him half of the people, the men [11] of the army. The (other) half of the people they shall not remove from their cities. If they conquer [12] their enemies and crush them and smite them with the sword, then take their booty, and [13] a tenth of it all shall be given to the king, a thousandth to the priests, and a hundredth to the Levites. [14] Half of the remainder they shall divide between those who took part in the war and their brothers [15] whom they left in their cities. If he goes out to war against [16] his enemies (*i.e. on the*

offensive), a fifth of the people shall go with him, the men of war, all able-bodied [17] men. And they shall guard themselves from every unclean thing and from every sexual transgression and from every iniquity and guilt. [18] And he may not go out before he has come before the High Priest and he has sought on his behalf the decision of the Urim [19] and of the Thummim; on his instructions he shall go out and on his instructions he shall return home, he and all the Israelites who [20] are with him. He may not go out of his own accord, before he has sought the decision of the Urim [21] and the Thummim. Thus he shall have success in all his ways, because he will have gone out according to the decision which

Column 59

[1] ... [2] ... in man[y] lands and ... [as] an example and as a proverbial mocker, and (suffer) under a heavy yoke [3] and under lack of everything. And they shall worship there other gods, the products of human hands (from) wood and stone, silver [4] and gold. And during all this, their cities shall become a waste land, a horrible place and a place of ruins, so that (even) [5] their enemies shall be horrified by them. They shall sigh in the lands of their enemies, [6] and cry loudly for help on account of the heavy yoke, and call, but I shall not hear; and they shall cry, but I shall not give an answer [7] to them, because of the evil of their deeds. And I shall hide my face from them so that they shall become (animal) feed [8] and plunder and booty without anyone to help, because of their wickedness, for they have broken my covenant [9] and their soul has scorned my Torah, until they burdened themselves with every guilt. Afterwards they shall turn [10] to me with all their heart and with all their soul, according to all the words of this Torah [11] and I shall save them from the hand of their enemies, and redeem them from the hand of those who hate them, and bring them [12] into the land of their fathers. I shall redeem them, and increase them, and rejoice over them. [13] I shall be their God, and they shall be my people. But the king whose [14] heart and eye has turned disloyally from my commandments shall have none who shall sit (after him) on the throne [15] of his fathers—never, for I shall disjoin his descendants from further rule over Israel for ever. [16] But if he walks in my statutes and observes my commandments, and does [17] what is right and good before me, then he shall not lack one of his sons to sit on the throne of the kingship [18] of Israel for ever.

And I shall be with him, and save him from the hand of those who hate him and from the hand [19] of those who seek to take his life, and I shall give all his enemies to him, so that he shall rule them [20] at his discretion, but they shall not rule him. I have set him above, and not below; at the beginning, [21] and not at the end; and he shall reign for a long time over his kingdom, he and his sons after him

Column 60

[1] . . . [2] and all their consecrated gifts and all their fir[stborn] which are male and all . . . [3] of their cattle and all their holy gifts which they dedicate to me, together with every ho[ly gift] [4] of their *hillulim* (*cf. Lev. 19.24*). And their tax contributions of birds, wild animals and fish shall be one thousandth [5] of what they catch and of everything that they have placed under a ban and (likewise) the tax on booty and spoil. [6] And to the Levites (is due) the tithe of corn and of (new) wine and fresh oil which [7] they have first dedicated to me (*cf. Num. 18.21*); further (provision of) the shoulder from the sacrifice is (the responsibility) of those who sacrifice. And the tax on [8] the booty and the spoil and the hunted game of birds, wild animals and fish shall be one hundredth, [9] but of the (wild) doves, as well as the tithe of (wild) honey, one fiftieth. But for the priests [10] one hundredth from the (wild) doves, for I have chosen them from all your tribes [11] to stand before me and to serve and to bless in my name, he and all his sons, constantly. [12] And if the Levite comes from one of your localities within the whole of Israel, in which [13] he dwells as a sojourner by his own desire, to the place that I choose to cause my name [14] to dwell, he shall serve like all his brother Levites who stand there before me. They shall eat equal [15] shares, except for proceeds inherited from the fathers. [16] When you enter the land that I give you, do not learn to [17] act according to the abominations of these peoples. Amongst you there shall not be found anyone making his son or daughter pass [18] through the fire, practising magic, conjuring spirits, soothsaying, practising witchcraft, uttering curses, enquiring of a ghost [19] or an oracular spirit, or enquiring (directly) of the dead, for they are an abomination before me, all who practise [20] these (things). Because of these very abominations I am driving them out from before you! [21] You shall be blameless in your dealings with YHWH, your God. For these people, who

Column 61

For line 2 see Yadin III, plate 39*, 1

[1] ... [2] Such a prophet shall be killed. And what if you shall say {to} in your heart, '[H]ow shall we recognize the word [3] which was not spoken by YHWH?' When the prophet speaks in the name of YHWH and the word is not realized [4] and does not come true, that is the word that I did not speak to him! The prophet said it presumptuously; do not be in awe [5] of him (*i.e. of killing him*). [6] A single witness may not appear against a man in any question of guilt or in connection with any crime that he has committed. The matter must rest on the basis (of the testimony) of two [7] witnesses or on the basis (of the testimony) of three witnesses. If a false witness appears against a man, to give [8] false evidence against him, the two men who have {the lawsuit} shall come before me and before the priests and before the Levites and before [9] the judges who will be there in those days, and the judges will conduct an investigation. If it happens that a witness has given false testimony, [10] falsely accusing his brother, then do to him what he had planned to do to his brother; thus you shall eradicate the evil from your midst. [11] And the others shall hear it and be afraid, so that they will not commit something of this sort in your midst again. Do not [12] show him any mercy: a life for a life, an eye for an eye, a tooth for a tooth, a hand for a hand, a foot for a foot! When [13] you go out to war against your enemies and you see horses and chariots and a force of men superior to you, then do not be afraid [14] of them, for I, who brought you up out of Egypt, am with you. And when you advance to battle, [15] the priest shall approach and speak to the people and say to them, 'Hear, Israel, you advance today

Column 62

For line 3 see Yadin III, plate 34*, 2

[1] ... [to] [2] home, ... [3] to speak to the people and say: 'Who is he who is afraid and faint-hearted? He shall go back to [4] his house, so that he does not weaken his brothers' heart like his own heart.' As soon as the judges (!) have finished [5] speaking to the people, they shall set troop commanders at the head of the people. When [6] you approach a city to fight against it, then you shall call upon it to

(make) peace. If [7] it answers you with an offer of peace and opens (its gates) to you, then all the people who are found in it shall be [8] tributaries to you and subservient to you. But if they do not make peace with you but declare war against you, [9] then besiege it and I shall give it into your hand. And you shall smite the male inhabitants with the edge of the sword; but [10] the women, the children and the cattle and all (property) which is in the city, all of its plunderable goods, you shall take as booty [11] for yourself, and you shall enjoy the spoil of your enemies that I give to you. So shall you do [12] with the cities that lie very distant from you, that are not from the cities of these peoples (here). [13] However, from the cities of the nations which I give you as an inheritance you shall leave nothing alive [14] of all the living creatures, but carry out the ban against the Hittites and the Amorites and the Canaanites, [15] the Hivites and the Jebusites and the Girgashites and the Perizzites, as I have commanded you, so that [16] they will not teach you to copy all the abominations, which they have made for their gods

Column 63

[1] ... wh[ich] ... [2] the heifer into the valley of a water-carrying stream, which has not been sown and not worked, and break the heifer's neck there. [3] Then the priests, the sons of Levi, shall approach, for I have chosen them to serve me and to bless in my name, [4] and so that every litigation and every symptom of leprosy shall be dealt with according to their decision. And all the elders of that city which is nearest to the slain person [5] shall wash their hands over the head of that heifer whose neck was broken in the valley. And they shall declare, 'Our hands [6] have not shed this blood and our eyes have seen nothing. Make atonement for your people Israel, that you have redeemed, [7] YHWH, and do not allow the guilt of innocent(ly shed) blood to remain in the midst of your people Israel.' And atonement shall be made for them for the blood. Thus you shall eradicate (the guilt of) [8] innocent(ly shed) blood, so that you do what is right and good before YHWH your God. [9] (*blank line*) [10] When you go out to war against your enemies and I give them into your hands, and you lead away their prisoners [11] and you see amongst the prisoners a woman of comely appearance, and desire her, and take her as a wife for yourself, [12] you shall bring her into your house and shave her head and cut her nails and remove [13] the clothes of her

captivity from her. And if she lives in your house for a month, and weeps for her father and her mother for a [14] month, then you shall afterwards go in to her and consummate the marriage, so that she becomes your wife. But she may touch nothing of yours that is (ritually) clean for [15] seven years and she may not eat the flesh of the *shelamim*-offering until seven years have passed. Afterwards she may eat

Column 64

For lines 2-3 see Yadin III, plate 34*, 4

[1] (*illegible remains of letters*) [2] If a ma[n] has a stubborn and rebellious [son] who does not listen (?) to the voice of his father or to the voice of his mother (?), [3] and they have chastised him, but [he] did not listen (?) to them, then his father and his mother shall take hold of him and bring him to [4] the elders of his city and to the gate (*i.e. the law-court*) of his place and say to the elders of his city, 'This son of ours is stubborn and [5] rebellious and does not listen to our voice; he is a wastrel and a drunkard'. Then all the men of his city shall stone him with stones, [6] so that he dies. Thus you shall eradicate the evil from your midst and all the Israelites shall hear and be afraid. If [7] a man passes on information about his people and betrays his people to a foreign people and does evil to his people, [8] then you shall hang him on the wood, so that he dies. On the strength of two witnesses or on the strength of three witnesses [9] he shall be killed and they shall hang him on the wood. If a man has committed a capital offence and flees to [10] the nations and curses his people, the Israelites, then you shall also hang him on the wood, [11] so that he dies. Yet they shall not let his corpse hang on the wood, but must bury it on the same day, for [12] cursed by God and men are those who are hanged on the wood, and you shall not pollute the earth, which I [13] give to you as an inheritance. If you see your brother's ox or his sheep or his ass, [14] when they have strayed, you shall not hide yourself from them (*i.e. him*). Bring them back to your brother and if your brother does not live near [15] to you and you do not know him, then take it (what you have found) into your house and it shall remain with you, until (he) asks

Column 65

See also Yadin III, plate 39*

¹⁻² . . . ³ young birds or eggs, and the mother bird is sitting on the
young birds(?) or on the eggs, ⁴ then you may not take the mother
with the young. You shall drive the mother away and ⁵ take the
young for yourself so t[hat] it will go well with you and you will live
long. When you build a new house, ⁶ you shall make a parapet on its
roof, so that you do not bring (the guilt of) blood(shed) onto your
house if someone falls ⁷ from it. If a man marries a woman and
consummates the marriage with her, but then does not like her (any
more) and lays blame on her ⁸ and spreads a false report about her,
saying, 'I took this woman and when I approached ⁹ her, I did not
find her to be a virgin', then the father of the young woman or her
mother shall take ¹⁰ the proof of the girl's virginity and bring it
before the elders of the gate. And the father of the girl shall say ¹¹ to
the elders, 'I have given my daughter to this man {as a wife} and now
he no longer likes her and he lays ¹² the blame for it on her, saying,
"I have found your daughter not to be a virgin". This (here) is the
proof of the virginity ¹³ of my daughter!' And they shall spread the
garment out before the elders of the city. Then the elders of this city
shall take ¹⁴ that man and chastise him and fine him a hundred
pieces of silver ¹⁵ and give them to the father of the girl. For that
man has spread a false report about a daughter of Israel. And to him

Column 66

¹ . . . of this city. . . . ² and they shall stone him with stones (?) [so
that] they will be killed, the girl because she did not cr[y] for help ³ in
the city and the man because he has violated his neighbour's wife.
Thus you shall eradicate ⁴ the evil from your midst. And if the man
found her {the woman} in the countryside at a place that is far and
not visible ⁵ from the city, and took her and lay with her, then only
the man who lay with her will be killed ⁶ and you shall do nothing to
the girl. The girl has brought no sin worthy of death upon herself, for,
as when a man ⁷ confronts his neighbour and kills him, so is this
case; for he found her in the countryside, and even if ⁸ the betrothed
girl had cried for help, there was no one there to help her. When a
man seduces a girl ⁹ who is a virgin and not betrothed, and if she is
permitted to him by law (as a wife) and he lies with her, ¹⁰ and is

discovered, then the man who lay with her shall give the father of the girl fifty pieces of silver, and she [11] shall become his wife because he violated her. He may not dismiss her during his lifetime. [12] A man may not take the wife of his father and he may not 'uncover the garment' of his father. A man may not take the wife [13] of his brother and may not 'uncover the garment' of his brother, the son of his father or the son of his mother, for it is a taboo of sexual impurity (for him). [14] A man may not take his sister, the daughter of his father or the daughter of his mother; it is an abomination. A man may not [15] take the sister of his father or the sister of his mother, for it is a disgrace. A man may not [16] take the [17] daughter of his brother or the daughter of his sister, for it is an abomination. A man may not take . . .

EXPLANATORY NOTES

Column 2

The beginning of this introduction, incorporating Ex. 34, will have been in col. 1, which has not been preserved. Here are given the instructions for building the Temple after entering the Holy Land—i.e. before the description in Ex. 35ff. of how the orders to establish the Tabernacle Sanctuary and its cult (Ex. 25ff.) were carried out. These instructions are included within the covenant mentioned in Ex. 34.10, and thus form part of the revelation at Sinai.

What remains shows a mixture of Ex. 34.10-13, Dt. 7.25-26 and Ex. 34.14-16, but with certain differences from the Masoretic text (MT). Thus, line 5 (Ex. 34.12) אליהם ('to them'); line 7 (34.13) ואת before פסילי; line 8 (Dt. 7.25) plural תחמודו; and line 9 adds תקח ממנו ממנו (based on Jos. 7.11? See Milgrom, *JQR* 71, 1); line 11 ו ('and') instead of MT כי ('for'); line 12 Ex. 34.15 begins with השמר ('take heed').

Columns 3–48

The overall layout of the Sanctuary

The Scroll construes the general Temple complex (Fig. 2) strictly according to the cultic principle of concentric areas of holiness, starting from the holiest centre and moving outwards through progressively lesser degrees of holiness (or purity). It further exploits the architectural layout so as to make a sharp division between the following areas:

Court I	the priests' area
Court II	the area for cultically qualified men
Court III	the area for ritually pure Israelites

It should be assumed that this entire complex lies in the centre of the 'Holy City'.

Just as the description in Ezek. 40ff. shows the gulf that had developed between the historico-architectural and topographical realities and the ritual conceptions of the monarchical period (i.e. in the First Temple) on the one hand, and the idealized conceptions of ritually minded priests on the other hand, so the Temple Scroll does the same thing for the period of the Second Temple. Its criticisms of the current Temple are nevertheless articulated in a unique fashion, not as prophetic revelation in the manner of Ezekiel, but as divine revelation to Moses—actually in direct imperative speech to Moses, as part of the Torah. Hence its stipulations are not for an eschatological future but for the historical period after the conquest of the Land. In other words, Solomon should actually have built the First Temple as it is described here in the Temple Scroll. What in fact he did build, and what was rebuilt on the model of the Solomonic Temple as the result of Cyrus's edict—and actually existed in a more or less altered form during the time of the author of the Scroll—was thus not built according to God's instruction and was therefore inadequate. Hence the harshest criticism of the current Temple was quite consistent with the strongest affirmation of the Temple cult. The outline which was back-dated in history (to Sinai) contains a carefully worked-out and well thought-through plan in which the utopian and the realistic are interwoven. Yet even the utopian did not lack a foundation in reality, because it aimed at solving problems which were acute in the Second Temple period; in particular, two: how are the areas of holiness correctly divided? and how, from the point of view of its layout, can a Temple intended for the whole of Israel be set up with functionally viable dimensions? The dimensions appear to go well beyond what was topographically feasible. But the extensions which King Herod made towards the south, with substantial infill and enclosing walls, also border on the astonishing and reflect similar concerns. With the large increase in population during the post-exilic period and the role of the Jerusalem Temple as (virtually) the only Jewish sanctuary, the traditional layout naturally came to be seen as more and more inadequate. In this respect the Scroll does not lie so far outside the framework of contemporary bias; it anticipates, in the form of an idealized sketch, what Herod in part realized. For the period after the conquest of the land, when no part of the city lay to the north and west of the present Temple area, the realization of the Temple Scroll's ideal would not have been topographically inconceivable. Whether it was technically feasible is a different, and even irrelevant, question.

The author of the outline, whose thought was dominated by priestly and cultic concerns, takes as his starting point the innermost area of holiness (or cultic activity) and surrounds it concentrically with progressively larger squares. The choice of a quadratic layout, as Yadin has observed, is not accidental, but corresponds to an old tradition which is already attested in Ezek. 40ff. Architecturally, the three areas mentioned above are so described that something like a four-sided portico emerges: closed courtyard constructions, consisting on each side of a gatehouse or gatehouses with side wings, so that the side structures would appear as an open porch on the inside. This porch either had the form of a stoa (pillared court)—a peristyle all the way round if a completely hellenistic model was followed—or it was built not with columns, but by extending and cutting through the dividing walls of the subsidiary buildings, which act like pillars to support the roof. This technique would correspond more closely to oriental building tradition. Courtyard design of this sort was very popular from the beginning of the hellenistic period onwards, even if the topographical factors rarely allowed complete symmetrical execution.

This type of design was, in principle, used in the formation of the agora, in the forum of large cities, in prestigious Roman villas and even in temple courts. As an idealistic schema not restricted by topographical considerations, the Scroll has the layout of the court-yards arranged uniformly on all sides. The reason for this is not so much an inclination towards architectural symmetry as a theological consideration. The author wanted to plan the Temple to be functionally viable for the twelve tribes, and therefore arranged the structures surrounding the Middle and Outer Courts so that each long side of the four-sided portico contained three gatehouses. Thus, gates were available on all sides for each of the twelve tribes of Israel (or sons of Jacob). In so doing, the gates were named in a specific sequence, and in this point the Scroll goes a long way beyond Ezekiel's plan.

The dimensions of the structures which surrounded the courtyard, and on which the proportions of the general layout depend, present a problem. It is to be assumed that in a plan for an ideal Temple the proportions will be carefully considered and symmetry will therefore be maintained. On this basis, there emerges not only a plausible reading of a number of details which diverges from that of Yadin, but a completely different overall interpretation. Admittedly, because of substantial loss of text, a number of measurements which would be indispensable for a complete reconstruction are missing. Thus, to a certain extent, the alternative to Yadin's reconstruction given below must remain hypothetical.

The principal data for the reconstruction of the general layout are as follows:

(1) A square Inner Court of 280 × 280 (= 7 × 40) cubits. According to Yadin (I, 154ff. [*I, 204ff.*]; II, 108f. [*II, 152ff.*]) this would be the *inside* measurement (since in 36.7 it is given as being 'from one inner corner to the other inner corner'), i.e. the square enclosed by the courtyard walls (whose thickness, according to Yadin's hypothesis, is 7 cubits). Thus the *outside* measurement would, according to Yadin, be 294 × 294 (280 plus 7 cubits for the thickness of each wall).

(2) A square Middle Court of 480 × 480 (= 12 × 40) cubits. According to Yadin this would be the *outside* measurement—the extent of the outer side of the court wall, including 4 cubits for the thickness of the walls.

(3) The width of the Middle Court as 100 cubits—but from where to where? There are exactly 100 cubits only if the two squares of 280 and 480 cubits *both* include the respective courtyard walls, making 100 cubits the distance between the *outside* of the wall of the Inner Court and the *outside* of the wall of the Middle Court. In Yadin's interpretation the distance would be from the *inside* of the one wall to the *outside* of the other, which is unlikely. This distance of 100 cubits is the weakest factor in Yadin's reconstruction, which no longer shows any symmetry, because to have 280 × 280 as an inner measurement and 480 × 480 as an outer measurement is inconsistent. Hence Yadin now computes the dimension of the Middle Court as 500 × 500 cubits instead of 480 × 480 (*I, 245, 414*).

(4) A square Outer Court of 1600 × 1600 (= 40 × 40) cubits. According to the individual specifications, the width of the gatehouses (50 + 50 + 50) plus 4 lengths of wall between the gatehouses and between gatehouses and corners (360 + 360 + 360 + 360) yields only 1590 cubits. Hence, Yadin is obliged to understand the figure of 1600 as an approximation. In this, the text offers him some support (see below). At any rate, Yadin also interprets this square of 1590 or 1600 cubits as an *outer* measurement, including 7 cubits for the thickness of the courtyard wall. The depth of the Outer Court from the outside of the wall of the Middle Court to the outside of the wall of the Outer Court would then be 1590 minus 480 (the length of the Middle Court) divided by 2, i.e. 555 cubits. And yet the figure for the depth of the Court in 40.7 apparently begins with the letter ש—which is not right for this number. However, the decisive point is that Yadin's

assumption meets with serious difficulties in the placing and subdivision of the buildings and porches of the enclosing structures, because shortening the Inner Court does not allow an equal configuration at each corner (Fig. 1c).

Yadin's *outer* measurements would thus be:

Inner Court 294 × 294
Middle Court 480 × 480 (or 500 × 500 to include the wall and the 'cells')
Outer Court 1590 × 1590 (or 1600 × 1600)

How did the 'architect' of the Scroll arrive at such apparently arbitrary measurements? No motive can be detected. The partial correspondence of the proportions of wall sections and overall lengths (120, 240, 360, 280, 360, 480), which Yadin stresses, proves little, since others (99 as the length of a section of wall in the Middle Court) do not fit this pattern.

If there is any underlying motivation it must be found in the relationship of the squares to one another. Now, that means that all three squares 280 × 280, 480 × 480, 1600 × 1600 (= 7 : 12 : 40 × 40) ought to be calculated on comparable measurements, not on a mixture of inner and outer dimensions.

Yadin explains that to take the length of the *inside* of the court wall together with the length of the *outside* of the court wall does not necessarily involve inconsistency, unless it is assumed that the author of the Scroll regarded the wall as an enclosing wall in the full sense of the word. However, even this explanation can create difficulties in the case of the Outer Court (see below). We are more likely to reach results if we examine the data from the point of view of the priestly author and with regard to the individual groups of buildings. From his priestly standpoint, the author of the layout is constantly looking from the inside towards the outside, in accordance with the general stance of the Scroll. He thinks first and foremost of its function vis-à-vis cult ritual, and the architecture serves to realize the idealized aims which derive from this standpoint. Looking from the inside towards the outside no measurement stands out—*except the length of the structures surrounding the courts*. It must remain an open question whether only the closed subsidiary buildings or also the open porch (whether stoa or peristyle) are to be included in the area of the surrounding structures. But this means that four portico-like structures surround each inner area. To maintain symmetry in this, we have to assume square corner buildings, which have the same width as the portico. Naturally, these corner structures either remained completely invisible from the inside or, if it was necessary in the porch, they projected so far into the courtyard corner that, at this point, they closed off the porches of the corner sections of the wall to form a 'stoa' (instead of forming a peristyle over the corner of the court).

On this assumption, all the lengths produced by the sum of the wall sections and gates of one side of a court are *de facto* the lengths of the court surfaces (and/or portico complexes) which were *accessible to pedestrians*, but not the outer or inner lengths of the court walls. The author was interested chiefly in these areas of the courts which were not built up, or which could be walked on. It was for *these* that he apparently wanted to arrive at specific proportions. It is therefore completely irrelevant whether—as is the case with the Inner Court—he specifies the length of sections of wall as being from 'gate to (inner) corner' or, as elsewhere, from 'gate to (outer) corner'. On both occasions it is the length of the portico part which is intended; the '(outer) corner' is both the (inner) corner of the court and the corner of the side complex of the court, but not the outer corner of the court itself. Thus, in the final analysis what is intended architecturally is 'from gate to corner structure'. This suggestion leads, with certain assumptions, to values for the outer lengths which are not haphazard, but rather betray conscious planning:

Court I
280×280 (7×40) cubits, court width or (inner) length of portico
300×300, outer square (including court wall)

Court II
480×480 (12×40) cubits, court width or length of portico
500×500 outer square (including court wall)
[500×500 is a traditional measurement in temple architecture (see below on 38.12ff.)]
100 cubits, depth of court, i.e. 500 minus 300 cubits (outer measurements of courts I and II) or 480 minus 280 cubits (inner measurements of courts I and II) divided by 2.

Court III
c. 1600×1600 (40×40) cubits, court width or length of portico complex, either accessible to those on foot or else not built on.

The length of the sides of the outer square depends
on the depth of the side-buildings + porticoes (see
below on 40.5ff.). A maximal value is given, since
the gatehouses project 36 cubits beyond the court
wall and into the court itself. The corner constructions therefore have maximal dimensions of 43 ×
43 (36 + 7 cubits for the thickness of the wall), and
by including the outward projections of the gates
and walls we reach a total of 50 × 50. The minimal
value would be an outside measurement of 1640 ×
1640 (Fig. 1a-b; 2) and the maximal value 1700 ×
1700.

All the figures provided by the Scroll, as well as the proportions,
are still in need of a thorough investigation in terms of architectural
history and number symbolism.

If the outer area for cult worship, around the Temple building and
the altar area within the Inner Court (Court I), was also supposed to
be formed in a square—which is to be assumed, against Yadin—then
it would have had the dimensions 200 × 200 (5 × 40). The 1600 ×
1600 square would be 8 × 8 of that, i.e. 64-fold.

Neither the division of the space within the Inner Court (or the
inner area for cult worship) nor the location of the individual
structures inside it can be established. Even the position of the
Temple building along the east-west axis is uncertain. If the inner
area for cult worship measured 200 × 200 cubits, one could conjecture
that it was located in the western half of the Inner Court, so that a
square of 100 × 100, which corresponds to the layout in Ezek. 40–48,
remained in front of the Temple building. In this 100 × 100 square,
probably in the centre, would have been the large altar for burnt-
offerings. To the south of it, probably directly opposite the altar and
its ramp, lay the store for the altar vessels (33.8ff.) and to the west of
it, at a distance of 7 cubits, the housing for the laver (31.1ff.). These
two equally large structures would occupy the area up to the line of
the frontage of the Temple building. Their gates suggest a ritual
'lock-gate' system; they lay on the boundary between areas of
holiness, either bordering on the 100 × 100 square of the altar area or
lying further to the south, on the edge of the 200 × 200 square, and,
depending on the position of the altar, at a distance of 50 cubits from
it. According to 35.8f. these structures were still in the area of highest
holiness, accessible only to priests on duty. A different matter is the

slaughtering facility, which is evidently to be situated to the north (cols. 34–35) and was also accessible to Levites (22.4, cf. Milgrom, *JBL* 97, 502f.). On that account it was possibly situated further to the north and outside the 200 × 200 square. The peristyle mentioned in 35.10ff. for sacrificial animals must then have lain outside the 200 × 200 square, which would anyway be the case if our assumption of this location for the Temple building is correct (though it must be borne in mind that the position of the Western gatehouse is uncertain). The remaining outer edge of the Inner Court, with a depth of 40 cubits, and the buildings surrounding the court, were thus accessible to Levites on duty in addition to priests. The situation is different in the description provided by Ezek. 40–48. Here the slaughtering facilities (40.38ff.) are attached to the northern gateway of the Inner Court which was accessible only to priests. They consist, moreover, of two slaughtering tables on the level of the Inner Court in the outer porch and two more slaughtering tables below on the level of the Outer Court, to the right and to the left of the steps. This division of slaughtering-tables may have the same underlying cause which in col. 35.10ff. brought about the stress on the partition in the peristyle, namely the strict separation between the sin-offerings for the people on the one hand, and for the priests on the other. An alternative solution, represented in Fig. 3 (p. 146) would place all the relevant structures in the 200 × 200 square, within which the area restricted to priests on duty would be separated off.

Columns 3–13.7

This section of the Scroll contains the stipulations for the actual Temple building and for the cult area of the altar. Unfortunately, not only is the text very badly preserved, but also the information is given in a comparatively terse fashion. This probably means that no particularly pressing concerns are at issue here and thus in the main the author takes up and repeats the biblical information (1 Kings 6–8) which, for its part, is also not very extensive where this central portion of the overall Temple layout is concerned.

Column 3

The specifications for the erection of the building and for the materials which were to be used in it extend as far as line 14, which is marked by a blank space deliberately left in the text. Line 2 calls to mind Ex. 35.6; line 3 could have been inspired by 2 Sam. 7.11 (cf. 1 Chron. 17.10). Yadin restores 'your enemies round about' (מסביב). This assumes a scribal error, for the letters before the lacuna are clearly מסי[. Lines 5-6 apparently warn against the use of materials from foreign parts—possibly a criticism aimed at Solomon's Temple. Line 9 mentions the *kapporet* ('cover') of the Priestly Code (Ex. 25.8 and frequently) above the Ark of the Covenant (col. 7.9). For the vessels see Yadin, I, 176f. (*I, 228ff.*). In line 11 מקדש clearly means the Priests' Court, the most holy area (see Milgrom, *JQR* 71, 1f.). The vessels provided for it could not be taken out of this area of holiness.

In lines 14ff., separated by the blank space mentioned above, are the details concerning the altar for the burnt-offerings. Mention is apparently made (cf. Yadin, I, 186 [*I, 239ff.*]), at least in the lines that have been preserved, to the 'brazen altar' (Ex. 27.4ff.; 38.1ff.), to which 1 Kings 8.64; 2 Chron. 4.1; Ezek. 9.2 may have given rise. How this 'brazen altar' is related to the great altar for burnt-offerings in col. 12.8 (see Yadin, II, 37 [*II, 47ff.*]) remains unexplained.

Column 4

The sparse remnants of text deal with the architectural specifications for the Temple building itself—in lines 1-6 apparently for the side-buildings (cf. 1 Kings 6.5-10; Ezek. 41.6ff.; Josephus, *Ant.* 8.70; *War* 5.220; Mishnah, *Middoth* 4.3-5). Mention is made of the terrace-like projections from the long-walls of the Temple building called רובד, on the inside of which the side-buildings with their (according to 1.5 six?) stories are supported. (For clarification see Yadin, I, 138f. [*I, 179f.*]). In line 4 it seems likely that an original יהי ('shall be') has been partly erased so that the first י has completely disappeared. This section is clearly separated from what follows because the rest of the line is blank.

Lines 7-14 concern the porch (אלם), the Temple hall (היכל) and the Holy of Holies, yet hardly anything has been preserved. In line 8 the verbal form באתה presents a puzzle. Yadin (*ad loc.*) conjectures a scribal error for ובניתה under the influence of Ezek. 40.48. But perhaps we have here a verb which is no longer preserved or which has coalesced with בנה 'build' (cf. J. Aistleitner, *Wörterbuch der ugaritischen Sprache*, Berlin 1965, 62, for the Ugaritic; also Ch.-F. Jean & J. Hoftijzer, *Dictionnaire des inscriptions sémitiques de l'ouest*, Leiden 1965, 45 under בתא in Palmyrene). The blank space of the rest of line 14 indicates that a new topic followed, which it is impossible to determine.

Columns 5–6

When the first part of the scroll, up to and including col. 5, was replaced with a section from the hand of the late Herodian scribe A, the text of the replacement section overlapped with the beginning of col. 6:

Overlapping of Text in Columns 5 and 6

5.5		]s with eight-and-twen[ty
6.3	e[ight-and-twent]y	cubit[s
5.6		]s and timberwork also
6.4	heig]ht for [ty]	cu[bit]s and timerwork[
5.7		]cubits is the total height
6.5		]ten cubits is the total height of the framework and the win[dow
5.8		to] it and four gates
6.6		fou]r gates to the upper storey on four [sides
5.9		]of the gate twelve[
6.7		t]welve [cubit]s and its [hei]ght one-[and-twenty
5.10-11	cubits and the whole framewo[rk	lo]wer and everything overlaid
6.8	]its doors [	] lower and everything[

5.13

A new section begins after the blank space at the end of line 12. Which 'portico' (פרור) this might be is no longer obvious. A פרור is a portico open on one side—a sort of stoa or peristyle (cf. Yadin, I, 34, 183f., 204f. [*I, 235f., 261ff.*]).

Column 7

Up to the blank space in line 13, this very badly preserved column (see the photographs in Yadin, III, plate 1*) apparently deals with the interior fittings of the Holy of Holies. Yadin (*ad loc.*; II, 18ff. and I, 139 [*II, 24ff.; I, 180*]) assumes that the figures for the planks required for the panelling of the room derive from Ex. 26.15, but have been adjusted to the larger Holy of Holies of the Solomonic Temple (1 Kings 6.15). Hence in line 5 'two-and-[eighty bo]ards' should be restored. Also, the details about the two Cherubim apparently come from Ex. 25.18ff. and have been put together with the data from the Solomonic Temple (1 Kings 6.23ff.; 8.7; 2 Chron. 5.8). Thus the Cherubim would stand face to face opposite one another as, in Yadin's opinion, lines 12-13 indicate (cf. Ex. 25.20).

For the rabbinic traditions about the use of gold in the preparation of the curtain discussed in lines 13ff. see Yadin *ad loc.* (II, 21 [*II, 27*]) and I, 139 (*I, 180*).

Column 8

After a blank space at the end of line 4 the cultic supply of shewbread is discussed (cf. Ex. 25.30). The comparatively extensive stipulations indicate a specific interest. The method, mentioned in lines 10 and 12, of putting the incense on the bread also runs counter to rabbinic tradition, as Yadin (*ad loc.*) shows.

Column 9

The very slight remains of the right-hand side of the column discuss the candelabrum in the Temple hall. Apparently only one is assumed, a *menorah* (seven-branched candelabrum) as in Ex. 25.31ff., such as was also found in the Second Temple, and which Josephus (*Ant.* 2.104) also assumes for the Solomonic Temple. Cf. Zech. 4.1-14;

Josephus, *Against Apion* 1.198 (Hecataeus of Abdera); 1 Macc. 1.21; 4.50; Josephus, *War* 5.216f.; the relief on the Arch of Titus in Rome.

Since the author of the Temple Scroll in part combines data from the tent sanctuary with data about the Temple, it is possible that he added 1 Kings 7.49 (10 candelabra: 5 in the north and 5 in the south) to this. Compare Eupolemus (B.Z. Wacholder, *Eupolemus*, 183f.); for 10 *menoroth*, each with seven lamps, see *Midrash Tadshe*, ed. A. Epstein, Vienna, 1887, xxvi.

Yadin (I, 140 and II, 30 [*I, 181f.; II, 39*]) reconstructs the text (according to MT and LXX) and gives prominence (II, 28f. [*II, 34ff.*]) to the fact that here two talents of gold are specified for all the vessels, including the *menorah*. Ex. 25.38f. presents ample opportunity for differing interpretations (cf. LXX, 1 talent; and see Yadin's references to rabbinic discussions).

In line 4, read מזה as the first word with Qimron, *Leshonenu* 42, 137: thus, three arms on the one side and three arms on the other. Cf. Milgrom, *JQR* 71, 2.

Line 5 ופרחיה; see Qimron, *ibid.*.

Column 10

Possibly the remains of the description of the Ulam curtain. Qimron (*ibid.*) has deciphered more. In line 5 לזכרון is to be read. According to Milgrom (*JQR* 71, 3-5), it concerns the precious metal tax; cf. Ex. 30.16; 4Q159, 6-7 and col. 39.9, below.

In line 10 Qimron (*ibid.* and *IEJ* 28, 162) reads מרים דף הולך תולע and remarks: 'If Yadin's hypothesis—that this passage deals with the drape covering the gates—is correct, the phrase דף הולך may be interpreted as a drape hung from a rod; but the lack of sufficient context leaves any interpretation doubtful'.

Column 11

See Yadin III, plate 5*. Unfortunately, this column, too, has been almost completely destroyed. From line 8 onwards it contains a catalogue of the feasts with the stipulations for the festal offerings. Yadin (*ad loc.* and I, 99 [*I, 128*]) suggests that in line 12 'and the six days [of the wood-offering]' is to be restored (on this see 23.9f.; 24.10-16; 43.3f.).

Column 12

Yadin (*ad loc.*) assumes that the discussion here is about the great altar for burnt-offerings (for this see also on 16.16f.; 23.12ff.; 37.4). Accordingly, the restoration of the beginning of line 13 follows Yadin.

Milgrom (*JBL* 97, 520) considers 2 Kings 16.14-15 to be the source for the two altars and refers to Ezek. 9.2. The position of the bronze altar would then be to the north of the great altar, in agreement with 2 Kings 16.14. Qimron (*Leshonenu* 42, 138) deciphers a few more letters.

Columns 13.8–29

The cycle of festivals and their offerings

The Scroll enables us to make a complete reconstruction of the Qumran community's cycle of festivals and its solar calendar, which is also attested in the book of Jubilees. For a better understanding of the text, the calendar is given here in its entirety without detailed discussion: 364 days per year and 52 weeks, with the year beginning on Wednesday 1 Nisan (March/April). On the extreme left is the running total of days of the year, followed by the day of the week, then the day of the month. The days of the festivals are printed in italics and, apart from the beginnings of the months and the Sabbaths, are described more precisely. Festivals of several days have the numbering of their days in bracketed Roman numerals. Sabbaths count as festivals in their own right and therefore, when they fall within a festal week, they are not counted as a day of the festival in question. To the right of *SAB* stands the running total of Sabbaths (and hence the number of the week) in brackets. On the extreme right, in brackets, are the running totals of days in the fifty-day periods between the festivals of first-fruits, in which the fiftieth day is also counted as the first day of the following period. In this way these festivals always fall on the first day after the seventh Sabbath, on a Sunday. Yadin provides a thorough discussion of the problem of the calendar (in Vol. I) and also refers to mediaeval sources which attest similar practices in Karaite tradition. To this should now be added J.L. Weinberger, *JQR* 68, 46-60.

I. NISAN

1) *Wed*	1. *I. (New Year)*	
2) *Thu*	2. *Consecration*	(I)
3) *Fri*	3.	(II)
4) *SAB(1)*	4.	
5) *Sun*	5.	(III)
6) *Mon*	6.	(IV)
7) *Tue*	7.	(V)
8) *Wed*	8.	(VI)
9) *Thu*	9.	(VII)
10) *Fri*	10.	(VIII)
11) *SAB(2)*	11.	
12) Sun	12.	
13) Mon	13.	
14) *Tue*	14. *Passover*	
15) *Wed*	15. *Mazzoth*	(I)
16) *Thu*	16.	(II)
17) *Fri*	17.	(III)
18) *SAB(3)*	18.	
19) *Sun*	19.	(IV)
20) *Mon*	20.	(V)
21) *Tue*	21.	(VI)
22) *Wed*	22.	(VII)
23) Thu	23.	
24) Fri	24.	
25) *SAB(4)*	25.	
26) Sun	26. *Sheaf waving*	
	First-fruits of	
	barley	
	Counting of the	
	Omer	(1)
27) Mon	27.	(2)
28) Tue	28.	(3)
29) Wed	29.	(4)
30) Thu	30.	(5)

II. IYYAR

31) *Fri*	1. *II*	(6)
32) *SAB (5)*	2.	(7)
33) Sun	3.	(8)
34) Mon	4.	(9)
35) Tue	5.	(10)
36) Wed	6.	(11)
37) Thu	7.	(12)
38) Fri	8.	(13)
39) *SAB (6)*	9.	(14)
40) Sun	10.	(15)
41) Mon	11.	(16)
42) Tue	12.	(17)
43) Wed	13.	(18)
44) Thu	14.	(19)
45) Fri	15.	(20)
46) *SAB (7)*	16.	(21)
47) Sun	17.	(22)
48) Mon	18.	(23)
49) Tue	19.	(24)
50) Wed	20.	(25)
51) Thu	21.	(26)
52) Fri	22.	(27)
53) *SAB (8)*	23.	(28)
54) Sun	24.	(29)
55) Mon	25.	(30)
56) Tue	26.	(31)
57) Wed	27.	(32)
58) Thu	28.	(33)
59) Fri	29.	(34)
60) SAB (9)	30.	(35)

III. SIVAN

61) *Sun*	1. *III.*	(36)
62) Mon	2.	(37)
63) Tue	3.	(38)
64) Wed	4.	(39)
65) Thu	5.	(40)
66) Fri	6.	(41)
67) *SAB (10)*	7.	(42)
68) Sun	8.	(43)
69) Mon	9.	(44)
70) Tue	10.	(45)
71) Wed	11.	(46)
72) Thu	12.	(47)
73) Fri	13.	(48)
74) *SAB (11)*	14.	(49)
75) *Sun*	15. Feast of	
	Weeks	(50)
	First-fruits of	
	wheat	(1)
76) Mon	16.	(2)
77) Tue	17.	(3)
78) Wed	18.	(4)
79) Thu	19.	(5)
80) Fri	20.	(6)
81) *SAB (12)*	21.	(7)
82) Sun	22.	(8)
83) Mon	23.	(9)
84) Tue	24.	(10)
85) Wed	25.	(11)
86) Thu	26.	(12)
87) Fri	27.	(13)
88) *SAB (13)*	28.	(14)
89) Sun	29.	(15)
90) Mon	30.	(16)
91) Tue	31.	(17)

IV. TAMMUZ

92) *Wed*	1. *IV.*	(18)
93) Thu	2.	(19)
94) Fri	3.	(20)
95) *SAB (14)*	4.	(21)
96) Sun	5.	(22)
97) Mon	6.	(23)
98) Tue	7.	(24)
99) Wed	8.	(25)
100) Thu	9.	(26)
101) Fri	10.	(27)
102) *SAB (15)*	11.	(28)
103) Sun	12.	(29)
104) Mon	13.	(30)
105) Tue	14.	(31)
106) Wed	15.	(32)
107) Thu	16.	(33)
108) Fri	17.	(34)
109) *SAB (16)*	18.	(35)
110) Sun	19.	(36)
111) Mon	20.	(37)
112) Tue	21.	(38)
113) Wed	22.	(39)
114) Thu	23.	(40)
115) Fri	24.	(41)
116) *SAB (17)*	25.	(42)
117) Sun	26.	(43)
118) Mon	27.	(44)
119) Tue	28.	(45)
120) Wed	29.	(46)
121) Thu	30.	(47)

End of the NISAN Period

V. AB

122) *Fri*	*1. V.*		(48)
123) *SAB (18)*	2.		(49)
124) *Sun*	*3. Wine Festival*	(50/1)
125) Mon	4.		(2)
126) Tue	5.		(3)
127) Wed	6.		(4)
128) Thu	7 .		(5)
129) Fri	8.		(6)
130) *SAB (19)*	9.		(7)
131) Sun	10.		(8)
132) Mon	11.		(9)
133) Tue	12.		(10)
134) Wed	13.		(11)
135) Thu	14.		(12)
136) Fri	15.		(13)
137) *SAB (20)*	16.		(14)
138) Sun	17.		(15)
139) Mon	18.		(16)
140) Tue	19.		(17)
141) Wed	20.		(18)
142) Thu	21.		(19)
143) Fri	22.		(20)
144) *SAB (21)*	23.		(21)
145) Sun	24.		(22)
146) Mon	25.		(23)
147) Tue	26.		(24)
148) Wed	27.		(25)
149) Thu	28.		(26)
150) Fri	29.		(27)
151) *SAB (22)*	30.		(28)

VI. ELLUL

152) *Sun*	*1. VI.*		(29)
153) Mon	2.		(30)
154) Tue	3.		(31)
155) Wed	4.		(32)
156) Thu	5.		(33)
157) Fri	6.		(34)
158) *SAB (23)*	7.		(35)
159) Sun	8.		(36)
160) Mon	9.		(37)
161) Tue	10.		(38)
162) Wed	11.		(39)
163) Thu	12.		(40)
164) Fri	13.		(41)
165) *SAB (24)*	14.		(42)
166) Sun	15.		(43)
167) Mon	16.		(44)
168) Tue	17.		(45)
169) Wed	18.		(46)
170) Thu	19.		(47)
171) Fri	20.		(48)
172) *SAB (25)*	21.		(49)
173) *Sun*	22. *Oil Festival*	(50)
174) *Mon*	23. *Wood Festival* (?)	(I)
175) *Tue*	24.		(II)
176) *Wed*	25.		(III)
177) *Thu*	26.		(IV)
178) *Fri*	27.		(V)
179) *SAB (26)*	28.		
180) *Sun*	29.		(VI)
181) *Mon*	30.		
182) *Tue*	31.		

End of the TAMMUZ period

VII. TISHRI

183) *Wed*   1. VII.
184) Thu   2.
185) Fri   3.
186) *SAB (27)* 4.
187) Sun   5.
188) Mon   6.
189) Tue   7.
190) Wed   8.
191) Thu   9.
192) *Fri*   10. Day of Atonement
193) *SAB (28)* 11.
194) Sun   12.
195) Mon   13.
196) Tue   14.
197) *Wed*   15. Feast of
              Tabernacles   (I)
198) *Thu*   16.   (II)
199) *Fri*   17.   (III)
200) *SAB (29)* 18.
201) *Sun*   19.   (IV)
202) *Mon*   20.   (V)
203) *Tue*   21.   (VI)
204) *Wed*   22.   (VII)
205) *Thu*   23.   (VIII)
206) Fri   24.
207) *SAB (30)* 25.
208) Sun   26
209) Mon   27.
210) Tue   28.
211) Wed   29.
212) Thu   30.

VIII. HESHVAN

213) *Fri*   1. VIII.
214) *SAB (31)* 2.
215) Sun   3.
216) Mon   4.
217) Tue   5.
218) Wed   6.
219) Thu   7.
220) Fri   8.
221) *SAB (32)* 9.
222) Sun   10.
223) Mon   11.
224) Tue   12.
225) Wed   13.
226) Thu   14.
227) Fri   15.
228) *SAB (33)* 16.
229) Sun   17.
230) Mon   18.
231) Tue   19.
232) Wed   20.
233) Thu   21.
234) Fri   22.
235) *SAB (34)* 23.
236) Sun   24.
237) Mon   25.
238) Tue   26.
239) Wed   27.
240) Thu   28.
241) Fri   29.
242) *SAB (35)* 30.

IX. KISLEV

243) *Sun*   1. *IX.*
244) Mon   2.
245) Tue   3.
246) Wed   4.
247) Thu   5.
248) Fri   6.
249) *SAB (36)*   7.
250) Sun   8.
251) Mon   9.
252) Tue   10.
253) Wed   11.
254) Thu   12.
255) Fri   13.
256) *SAB (37)* 14.
257) Sun   15.
258) Mon   16.
259) Tue   17.
260) Wed   18.
261) Thu   19.
262) Fri   20.
263) *SAB (38)* 21.
264) Sun   22.
265) Mon   23.
266) Tue   24.
267) Wed   25.
268) Thu   26.
269) Fri   27.
270) *SAB (39)* 28.
271) Sun   29.
272) Mon   30.
273) Tue   31.

X. TEBET

274) *Wed*   1. *X*
275) Thu   2.
276) Fri   3.
277) *SAB (40)*   4.
278) Sun   5.
279) Mon   6.
280) Tue   7.
281) Wed   8.
282) Thu   9.
283) Fri   10.
284) *SAB (41)* 11.
285) Sun   12.
286) Mon   13.
287) Tue   14.
288) Wed   15.
289) Thu   16.
290) Fri   17.
291) *SAB (42)* 18.
292) Sun   19.
293) Mon   20.
294) Tue   21.
295) Wed   22.
296) Thu   23.
297) Fri   24.
298) *SAB (43)* 25.
299) Sun   26.
300) Mon   27.
301) Tue   28.
302) Wed   29.
303) Thu   30.

End of the TISHRI period

XI. SHEBAT			XII. ADAR		
304) *Fri*	*1. XI.*		334) *Sun*	*1. XII.*	
305) *SAB (44)*	2.		335) Mon	2.	
306) Sun	3.		336) Tue	3.	
307) Mon	4.		337) Wed	4.	
308) Tue	5.		338) Thu	5.	
309) Wed	6.		339) Fri	6.	
310) Thu	7.		340) *SAB (49)*	7.	
311) Fri	8.		341) Sun	8.	
312) *SAB (45)*	9.		342) Mon	9.	
313) Sun	10.		343) Tue	10.	
314) Mon	11.		344) Wed	11.	
315) Tue	12.		345) Thu	12.	
316) Wed	13.		346) Fri	13.	
317) Thu	14.		347) *SAB (50)*	14.	
318) Fri	15.		348) Sun	15.	
319) *SAB (46)*	16.		349) Mon	16.	
320) Sun	17.		350) Tue	17.	
321) Mon	18.		351) Wed	18.	
322) Tue	19.		352) Thu	19.	
323) Wed	20.		353) Fri	20.	
324) Thu	21.		354) *SAB (51)*	21.	
325) Fri	22.		355) Sun	22.	
326) *SAB (47)*	23.		356) Mon	23.	
327) Sun	24.		357) Tue	24.	
328) Mon	25.		358) Wed	25.	
329) Tue	26.		359) Thu	26.	
330) Wed	27.		360) Fri	27.	
331) Thu	28.		361) *SAB (52)*	28.	
332) Fri	29.		362) Sun	29.	
333) *SAB (48)*	30.		363) Mon	30.	
			364) Tue	31.	

End of the TEBET period

13.8-16
This discussion of the regular offering (*Tamid*) begins with the morning offering (lines 8-13); then it mentions the hide of the sacrificial animal as a portion for the priests (lines 13f.) and concludes with the evening *Tamid*.

At line 16 begins an apparently definitive prohibition, for which Yadin, in the light of CD 6.11-14, suggests a restoration according to Mal. 1.10 ('And do not light my altar in vain'); but this is questionable.

13.17
After the blank space at the end of line 16 began the regulations for the Sabbath offering which, as with all festal offerings, is to be brought in addition to the *Tamid*. The form of the underlying text, Num. 28.9f., stands close to that behind the LXX ('Sabbaths', 'you shall offer').

14.?-8
The offering for the first of the month: cf. Num. 28.11ff., which Yadin (II, 43) uses for his reconstruction.

14.9ff.
For the particulars of the offering for the first day of the first month (= Nisan!) and thus for the New Year Festival, the Scroll employs an abbreviated and transposed form of the text of Num. 29.1ff. (cf. Yadin, I, 74 [*I, 89*]). As Yadin observes (I, 114f. [*I, 143f.*]), here as elsewhere (cf. 14.18; 15.9, 17f.; 17.13-15; 18.4-6; 23.11f.; 25.5f., 12-15; 26.5-9; 27.3-5) a dual concern of the Scroll with regard to the sin-offerings becomes clear: they are to be offered before the burnt-offerings (thus not only their blood is to be sprinkled beforehand as Mishnah, *Zebaḥim* 10.2, indicates); and they are also connected with cereal- and drink-offerings. According to Yadin, the biblical basis for these precepts is chiefly Lev. 5.8; 8.14-18; Num. 8.12 and Ezek. 43.23.

In lines 16-18, the text is read according to Qimron, *Leshonenu* 42, 138 and *IEJ* 28, 162.

15.3–17.5

The Consecration

Immediately after the New Year Festival follows a festival of consecration, the rites of which are derived from Lev. 8.14 and Ex. 29.1ff. (cf. also the Temple consecration in 1 Kings 8; 1 Chron. 29.17; Ezek. 43.18ff.) but which also served for the annual consecration of the priests and, when necessary, for the consecration of the High Priest. Yadin (I, 75ff., 110ff. [*I, 90ff., 137ff.*]) refers to traces of a festival of this sort in rabbinic texts. Apparently a *Tamid* offering was not to be brought during this week of consecration.

Milgrom (*JBL* 97, 509f.) points out that apparently only that part of the rite which was controversial at the time is discussed here, namely Ex. 29.22-25 / Lev. 8.25-28. The Scroll interprets Ex. 29.24 (Lev. 8.27) as follows: 'And you shall place (and he placed) all these on the palms of Aaron and on the palms of his sons and designate them (he designated them) as an elevation offering'. Moses therefore commanded the *tenufah*-rite; the priests carried it out. Line 4 makes Lev. 21.10-15 more precise: the prohibition is operative for life.

16.12 goes beyond Lev. 4.12 and requires that the parts of the sin-offering be burned in a stipulated place. Milgrom (*ibid.*, 511ff.) draws attention to the fact that this question remained controversial for a long time (see the Babylonian Talmud, *Zebaḥim* 104b). And finally the Scroll stresses that cereal- and drink-offerings are a part of the sin-offering.

17.6-9

Passover

Cf. Lev. 23.5; Num. 9.2-5; 28.16; Dt. 16.1ff. The following points are striking, as Yadin I, 79-81 (*I, 96-99*) points out:

(1) the appointed time of the Passover slaughtering, which was not fixed in Ex. 12.6 and Dt. 16.6, is specified here as before the evening *Tamid*, with Jubilees 49.10 (cf. also 2 Chron. 35.11-14), and against rabbinic tradition.

(2) the age limit of twenty years also corresponds to Jubilees (49.17).

(3) according to Yadin's reconstruction in 17.8 the Passover meal was to be eaten during the night (cf. Ex. 12.8; Dt. 16.4) and the departure was to take place early the next morning (cf. Dt. 16.7).

(4) in line 9 the regulations for eating the Passover meal in the Temple Courts are made more specific than in Dt. 16.7, but cf. also Jubilees 49.

See G. Brin, *Shnaton* 4, 186, who notes the 'mosaic-like' use of Num. 9.3 (cf. LXX: first month!); Ex. 12.47; 12.8 and Dt. 16.7 in these lines.

17.10-16

The Feast of Mazzoth (Unleavened Bread)

Cf. Lev. 23.6-8; Num. 28.17-25; Jubilees 49. According to Brin, *Shnaton* 4, 186-90, the two biblical 'base texts' (with transpositions) are supplemented with the contents of Ezra 6.22f.; Num. 29.18 and Dt. 16.8. The stress lies on the goat of the sin-offering in Num. 29.18.

Column 18
Cf. Yadin, III, plate 20*, 2.

18.?-10

The Waving of the Omer

Cf. Lev. 23.10-14; Num. 28.26-31. The appointed time of this festival follows immediately on the seventh day of the Feast of Mazzoth, i.e. on the 26th of Nisan. It is defined as a festival of first-fruits for barley (see Yadin, I, 82ff. [*I, 100ff.*]).

18.10b–19.9

Counting of the Omer and Feast of Weeks

Cf. Lev. 23.15-21; Num. 28.26-31. See also 4QHal^a 5 (*DJD*, III, 300, in addition to 250, n. 122). The translation follows Yadin's restoration, but lines 14/15 are restored differently by Milgrom (*JQR* 71, 6-8): [שני תאפינה חלות] ('two wheat breads [baked into loaves, two] tenths') or: [שני תאפינה חמץ] ('two wheat breads [baked with leaven, two] . . . ').
   The counting of the fifty days begins with 26th Nisan. The fiftieth day falls on the Sunday after the seventh Sabbath according to this calendar. (In rabbinic practice the Counting of the Omer begins on the day after the first Sabbath after the Feast of Mazzoth.) This feast has a double character as the Feast of Weeks and as the Festival of

First-fruits for Wheat (more detailed discussion in Yadin, I, 84ff. [*I, 103ff.*]). It is noteworthy that despite Jubilees 6.17ff., no reference is made here to the Feast of Weeks as a celebration of the conclusion of the covenant. Apparently the description of the festival of first-fruits lay closest to the author's heart.

19.11–21.10

The Wine Festival

See Yadin, I, 88-90 (*I, 108-11*). On the fiftieth day after bringing the new cereal-offering (Festival of First-Fruits for Wheat), i.e. on the Sunday after the seventh Sabbath, the bringing of the new wine for the drink-offering is celebrated (cf. 43.7-9 and Jubilees 32.12ff.). This is *tiroš*, 'young wine', and not unfermented grape juice. The stipulations for the contributions of each tribe were twelve rams, corresponding to the twelve tribes (cf. 19.15f.), with the first-fruits offering according to Num. 28.26ff., and fourteen lambs as *shelamim*-sacrifices (20.1ff.), with the contribution of the priests' heave portion (20.14ff.). This made fourteen rams and fourteen lambs in all. The author set particular value on the description of the rite, which took place when the new wine was first drunk—a festive sacrificial meal in the courts of the Temple for priests, Levites and laity in order of rank. This was clearly also the model for the ritual meals of the Qumran community in their separation from the Jerusalem Temple. Cf. also Isa. 62.9 and J. Maier, *ZAW* 91, 125.

20.3-4
The translation follows the reading of Qimron, *Leshonenu* 42, 140.

20.10
Milgrom (*JQR* 71, 8f.) argues that for the formulation Num. 5.15 and Lev. 5.11 (cf. 6.8) are applicable, rather than Lev. 7.10.

For 20.15ff. see also Milgrom (*JBL* 97, 504ff.) on 60.7. In 20.15ff. and Rockefeller Museum fragment 43.975, line c, which Yadin uses to restore the text between columns 20 and 21, precise detail is given about the priestly portion of the sacrifice: the אזרוע/זרוע does not include the shoulder. As Milgrom (in Yadin, I, 131-36) makes clear, for anatomical reasons, when the extremities were removed from the sacrificed animal, the forequarters generally included the shoulder,

and the hindquarters the haunches. Ancient oriental graphic represent-
ations also show this. Only in a second operation can the shoulder (or
the haunch) be removed. In 60.6-7 it becomes clear why the priestly
portion is described so precisely: the shoulder is in fact the portion
for the Levites—a hitherto unrecognized ruling which, according to
Milgrom, developed from Dt. 18.3. The question is, whose responsibility was this levitical portion, that of the priests (cf. Yadin, I, 119ff.
[*I, 151ff.*]) or that of the laity (Milgrom)? 60.6-7 (cf. *ad loc.*) argues
for the latter, for the shoulder is there described as being provided by
the זובחי הזבח, 'those who sacrifice'.

21.2 is read with Qimron, *Leshonenu* 42, 140: אחר לכול הממן[. Did
the tribe of Levi also receive, in addition to their own portion, a
portion in pursuance of their levitical functions? Cf. on this Milgrom,
JBL 97, 501 and 519 as well as 22.11-13.

On 21.8-9 see Milgrom, *JQR* 71, 9 (cf. Jubilees 7.1-6).

21.12–23.9

The Fresh Oil Festival

The fresh oil (יצהר) was to be used in the Temple for cereal-offerings
and for the candelabrum on the day when it was offered, namely the
fiftieth day (the Sunday following the seventh Sabbath) after the
Wine Festival. As with the new wine, in this cultic calendar the new
oil was pointedly brought into the foreground, clearly in contrast to
other practice at that time. In general the form of the Oil Festival was
like that of the Wine Festival. A celebratory first-fruits rite, based on
analogy with the wine-drinking rite was contained in the text. For
details, cf. Yadin, I, 91ff.

22.d
Milgrom, *JQR* 71, 15f. finds two types of atonement offering.

22.3
Milgrom (*JBL* 97, 518f.) reconstructs differently from Yadin: א[י]לים,
'fourteen rams'. He refers to 29.1-2, where he restores similarly.
These would be the fourteen rams and lambs of the *shelamim*-
offering, consumed by priests and Levites in the Outer Court (21.e-3;
22.11-13). 22.4 assigns the task of slaughtering to the Levites. Was
this usually the case (cf. Ezek. 44.10f.; 2 Chron. 30.17; 35.6, 10f.)? Cf.

Milgrom, *JBL* 97, 502f. Also surprising is the use of בני לוי—the normal expresion in the Scroll for the members of the tribe of Levi—instead of הלויים (cf. also B. Thiering, *JBL* 100, 63).

22.9

Milgrom (*JBL* 97, 504f.) queries Yadin's reading and interpretation of ולראשית: according to Dt. 18.3 מנה could not refer to the flesh of a sacrifice, nor ראשית to the foreleg. But see Yadin's criticism, *I, 411*.

22.10

Reading וללויים before the lacuna at the end, with Qimron, *Leshonenu* 42, 141.

22.11-13

This stresses that the *shelamim*-offerings are the property of the laity (Milgrom, *JQR* 71, 9f.).

22.14–23.2

According to D. Rokeah (*Shnaton* 4, 266ff.), we might compare Josephus, *War* 2.123ff.

22.15f.

Cf. 21.7-9 and Lev. 16.30-34. Milgrom (*JQR* 71, 10f.) interprets כפר ('atone') here as desacralization: the first-fruits were permitted for profane consumption. The object of טהר is at the same time the means of כפר.

23.?–25.2

The Wood Festival

In the lost upper part of col. 23 began the specifications for the wood-tribute to the Temple, which are extremely idiosyncratic and historic-ally interesting. According to Yadin's reconstruction and interpretation of the text (I, 99ff. [*I,122ff.*]) it was (as perhaps 11.12 also suggests) a six-day festival, cf. also 43.4. Wood-tributes are mentioned in e.g. Neh. 10.35 and 13.31, but on different fixed dates. Rabbinic literature names nine such dates (Mishnah, *Ta'anit* 4.5; cf. Tosephta, *Bikkurim* 2.9). From the literature of Qumran, CD 11.18f. should be cited, but this reference provides nothing more specific. Perhaps Josephus, *War*

2.425, also assumes a single fixed date (thus Yadin), but this need not be the case, for Josephus mentions this feast at a specific date (14th Ab?) only in passing, and thus does not exclude the possibility of other dates. Rather, it is Jubilees 21.13f. which offers a possible analogy, in so far as its requirement not to use any 'old wood' for the altar is to be understood in the context of the regulations for the festival of first-fruits: nothing more of the old could be used beyond the appointed annual date. According to Yadin (I, 105 [*I, 130ff.*]) the Scroll concentrates the wood-tributes into the period immediately following the Oil Festival, by analogy with the first-fruits festivals. The place of the Wood Festival immediately after the Oil Festival does appear to be fixed in the calendar; but if so, since the next festival follows on 1st Tishri, there can hardly be any solution other than Yadin's: the first day of the wood festival fell on 23rd Ellul, the last on the 29th (the 28th, being a Sabbath, is not counted). An alternative suggestion would be that this occasion is only the *first* appointed wood-offering, with which a *cycle* of 6 wood-offerings would open.

Each day/date was intended for 2 tribes, as listed in the order of offerings:

1. date/day: Levi and Judah
2. date/day: Benjamin and the sons of Joseph
3. date/day: Reuben and Simeon
4. date/day: Issachar and Zebulun
5. date/day: Gad and Asher
6. date/day: Dan and Naphtali

Yadin (*I, 408f.*) refers to Gen. 46.8ff.; the enumeration there is modified here by arranging the tribes and their offerings in pairs. Apparently Ezek. 43.18ff. and Num. 7 (cf. 1QM 2) also served as models, whereby in accordance with Qumran ideology, the priestly tribe of Levi stood at the head, before the royal tribe of Judah, followed by Benjamin. These three tribes represented the actual constitution of the nation at the author's time but, since he is describing the Temple and its cult in the past when the people had consisted of twelve tribes, he adds the 'lost' ten tribes. The Mishnah assumes only the first three tribes—those who actually existed at the time—and divides the dates according to the priestly families. The relationship of the sequence of these groups of paired tribes to the order of the names given for the gates of the Middle and Outer

Courts of the Temple is interesting. Here we come across the following arrangement:

Levi and Judah	(in the east)
Joseph and Benjamin	(in the south)
Zebulun and Issachar	(in the west)
Dan and Naphtali	(in the north)
Simeon and Reuben	(south-east corner, separated by Levi and Judah)
Gad and Asher	(north-west corner, separated by Dan and Naphtali)

There is thus a certain coherence. (See further on 40.13ff.) Milgrom (*JQR* 71, 12ff.) classifies 23.3-10 as 'prescriptive administrative order' and 23.11ff. as 'descriptive procedural order'; cf. the ritual for Yom Kippur, 25.12ff.

23.12-13
Instead of Yadin's restoration, we read ונתן מדמו and יסוד with Qimron, *Leshonenu* 42, 141.

23.13f.
Cf. Ezek. 43.20 and Lev. 4.25: here they are harmonized.

23.15
According to Milgrom, *JQR* 71, 15, עם הכליות corresponds to . . . על, 'in addition to the kidneys'; cf. Lev. 3.15.

Column 24
Additional readings are provided by Qimron, *Leshonenu* 42, 141.

24.7f.
Note the polemical stress on the prescription that cereal- and drink-offerings must always come to the altar with the pertinent sacrifices (cf. Yadin, I, 118).

24.8
Yadin reads ואדביה as the first word and takes אדב as the designation of a particular part of the body of the sacrificial animal. But the reading אדביה is also justifiable. The root is attested in the Bible at least as a verbal form (1 Sam. 2.33) and in the proper name *'Adbe'el* (W. Baumgartner, *Hebräisches und Aramäisches Lexikon zum Alten Testament*, fasc. 1, Leiden, 1967, 11). Possibly אדב is the designation

for prepared parts of animal sacrifices. Hence, in the case of sacrifices, the verb might mean 'to invite to the meal'. Milgrom (*JQR* 71, 89) suggests reading אברית, 'so shall they do to each bull, ram and lamb: its sections shall remain apart'.

25.2-10

The First Day of the Seventh Month

In the rabbinic calendar this is the New Year. With these lines, which are only preserved in a very fragmentary state, compare Lev. 23.23 with Num. 29.1-6 and Ezek. 45.18-21, as well as Josephus, *Ant.* 3.239.

25.10–27.10

The Day of Atonement

Cf. Lev. 16; 23.27-32 and Num. 29.7-11. The biblical texts are here skilfully combined (for details see Yadin I, 106ff. [*I, 131ff.*]). The number of rams, uncertain on the basis of the biblical text, is now stipulated: there are three (in rabbinic texts, two), one for the burnt-offering and two for the sin-offering (one for the High Priest, one for the people). Cf. Josephus, *Ant.* 3.240-43. Moreover, the order of the ritual is given precisely: first the sin-offering: (1) one young bull (cf. Lev. 4.8ff.), (2) the first goat and washing of the High Priest, (3) the second goat; then the burnt offering.

27.5

The division of sentences follows Yadin's reading, יהיה. Qimron (*IEJ* 28, 170) suggests והיו on the basis of Lev. 16.24 and Ex. 12.14 and thus takes the phrase with the preceding clause.

27.10–29.2/3

The Feast of Tabernacles

See also 11.13; 42.10ff.; 44.6ff. Cf. Lev. 23.33-36; Num. 29.12-38; Ezek. 45.25 (23-25) and Yadin, I, 108f. (*I, 131ff.*). The prescriptions contain nothing surprising, if one overlooks the Scroll's characteristic placing of the sin-offering before the burnt-offering. But compare

28.4-9 with Num. 29.19-22: Yadin (I, 114 [*I, 143*]) notes that the ancient versions attest differing textual traditions for this passage. For a reconstruction of the text of col. 29 see Yadin II, 89-91 (*II, 125ff.*).

29.2/3–30.?

Conclusion of the Prescriptions for the Festivals

Lines 8-10 assume unequivocally that the Temple building described in the Scroll was for the period after the conquest of the Land and not as a sanctuary for the final days, supposedly lasting until the eschaton, the 'Day of Blessing'. The view, most recently represented by B. Thiering (*JBL* 100, 60f.), that the Scroll describes the Temple for the final days, is without foundation; see Yadin, *I, 412*. B.Z. Wacholder, *The Dawn of Qumran*, 21ff., also shares the opinion that the eschatological Temple is intended; עד (29.9) is understood as 'during'. Wacholder has also quoted the positions of Yadin and Maier incorrectly. For the period of salvation, God will 'create' (ברא) a new Temple and indeed one which would last forever; cf. for further details Yadin, I, 140-44 (*I, 182ff.* and *ad loc.* where he also discusses the relationship with Jubilees, in particular 1.17, 27).

For the covenant with Jacob at Bethel (Jub. 1.10), cf. the formulation of Lev. 26.42. The actual basis is, of course, Gen. 28.10-22; 35.1-15. Yet in Jubilees 32 the installation of Levi as priest and the disposition of the cultic tributes (in accordance with what was marked out in the 'heavenly tablets') are linked with Jacob's stay at Bethel. Thus the covenant with Jacob is not so concerned with the building of the Temple, against Yadin, who thinks particularly of Jubilees 32.16 where Jacob completes the building of a sanctuary at Bethel.

A comparison should also be made with 5Q13 2.6 (*DJD* III): ' . . . to Jacob you made known at Bethel . . . ', which Yadin restores to ' . . . at Bethel your covenant'. Since the fragments of 5Q13 also contain instructions relevant to the cult, the establishment of 'correct' regulations for the cult was traced back specifically to the covenant with Jacob where they were linked with the eschatological promise of a Temple created directly by God. They were thus made to pre-date the Sinai covenant. Jubilees ascribes in this way the origin of a great deal of biblical law and custom to the patriarchal era.

29.7

Reading with Qimron (*Leshonenu* 42, 142) נדריהמה instead of נסכיהמה;
cf. Lev. 23.38.

29.7/8

Brin (*Shnaton* 4, 220f.) considers whether YHWH can be seen in אהיה
('I shall be'). Cf. also 59.13.

29.9

'Blessing', reading ברכה, but it is difficult to be certain. Qimron reads
בריה = בריאה 'creation'.

30.?–36.?

The Buildings in the Outer Area for Cult Worship

After the treatment of the festivals and their offerings, which the
author has inserted after the instructions for the altar, he turns to the
subsidiary buildings in the outer area for cult worship.

30.3–31.9

The fragmentary text still allows us to recognize (cf. Yadin's reconstruction *ad loc.* and I, 163ff. [*I, 210ff.*]) that two different parts of
the Temple structure are dealt with here: (a) a staircase tower with a
square ground-plan, at a distance of 7 cubits to the north-west of the
Temple building. The steps lead up in the tower around a square
central pillar and into a passage to (b) the upper storey of the Temple
(or onto the roof of the Temple). מסיבה is thus a flight of steps on the
principle of the spiral staircase, but here four-cornered.

30.1-5

Qimron (*Leshonenu* 42, 142) reads somewhat more than is offered in
the translation. In particular, he adds another line between lines 3
and 4: ' . . . a step . . . [w]hich you should build . . . '.

30.10

The text is corrected according to Qimron (*ibid.*): . . . אמות [לכול] רוהותיו
ורוחב המסבה עולה מעלות ארבע.

31.4

At the end is mentioned the deputy of the High Priest, הכוהן המשנה; cf. 1QM 2.1.

31.10–33.7

The Housing for the 'Bronze Sea'

For details see Yadin, I, 168ff. (*I, 217ff.*). The 'Bronze Sea' of 1 Kings 7.23-26 (cf. also B.Z. Wacholder, *Eupolemus*, 190ff.; Mishnah, *Middoth* 3.6 and *Tamid* 1.4) here in the Scroll receives its own building, בית הכיור, to the south-west of the south side of the Temple building. Its dimensions are 21 × 21 cubits outside, 15 × 15 inside, 20 cubits high with a gate 4 cubits wide and 7 cubits high on its eastern, northern and western sides. On the inside, recesses were set into the walls, probably for clothing to be deposited (Yadin, I, 171, refers to the wall recesses at Massada). Around the wall of the housing runs a channel that draws off water into a shaft reaching into the earth, because the Scroll advocates that, ritually speaking, water draining off and partially mixed with blood is to be regarded as blood and should not be touched. This has nothing to do with Ezek. 47.1 (against Yadin) where the concern is with the supply of water.

Improved readings according to Qimron are: line 11 הקן[י]ר (*IEJ* 28, 164); line 12: . . . שרים אמה [ע]; line 13: רוחב (*Leshonenu* 42, 143).

32.1-10
Improved readings are given in Qimron, *ibid.*

33.6
Reading with Qimron אל הכיור ויוצאים.

33.8–34.?

The House for the Altar Vessels

For details and sketches see Yadin, I, 174ff. (I, 224). While the Mishnah knows of two separate but identically described rooms for the vessels (*Tamid* 3.4 for altar vessels, *Sheqalim* as a sort of collection point for contributions) and provides a place in the Temple vestibule (*Ulam*) for the sacrificial knives (*Middoth* 4.7), Josephus

(*Ant.* 3.150) situates a separate structure for the vessels opposite the altar. This comes close to the Scroll which puts a building for the vessels to the north of the housing for the laver and gives it the same dimensions, but with only two gates (in the south and north) and, on the inside, makes it full of recessed storage in the walls.

On the Temple vessels see Yadin, I, 176ff. and cf. on 3.8ff.

33.8
An improved reading is given in Qimron, *Leshonenu* 42, 143.

33.14
Reading with Qimron (*Tarbiz* 52, 133) and Yadin (*I, 419; II, 143*) ולכוננות, 'bowls' (?).

34.?–35.?

The Slaughtering Site

See the introduction to cols. 3–48 above. Since, according to 22.4, it was the Levites who did the slaughtering, the site would lie outside the altar area (so Yadin, *I, 413*). For details see Yadin, II, *ad loc.* and I, 178ff., 297 [*I, 238ff., 388*].

To the north of the altar a structure of twelve columns fitted with beams was to be set up. A similar device for hoisting the sacrificial animals is mentioned in Mishnah, *Middoth* 3.5 (cf. *Tamid* 3.5), in this case with eight columns and six rows each with four 'rings' corresponding to the twenty-four priestly courses. The animals were apparently placed with their necks or heads in 'rings' (cf. Mishnah, *Pesaḥim.* 5.19; Yadin also quotes a mediaeval text, Abraham b. Azriel, *Sefer Arugat ha-Bosem*, ed. E. Urbach, I, Jerusalem, 1939, 61). The animals were probably lifted by their hind-legs with a sort of hoist; this procedure was necessary to allow for bleeding. Then they were placed in these rings, through which it was possible to pull the head by means of a locking traction mechanism so that they could be slaughtered easily. After slaughter and bleeding, the bar of the 'wheels' was released and the animals hung ready for skinning and cutting up. Yadin (I, 181, 297 [*I, 234, 338*]) indicates the possibility that the method of suspending the sacrificial animal described in the rabbinic sources, as in the Scroll, goes back to John Hyrcanus, who introduced a similar method after the transfer of power to the Sadducean party. The influence of this practice on the Scroll is less probable than that of a common older practice underlying both descriptions, one which had already been the subject of debate for some time. In other respects the difference between the Scroll and the relevant rabbinic texts is comparatively slight.

34.13

Qimron (*Leshonenu* 42, 144) reads וממנו ('and from him') instead of ושמנו ('and his oil'). This would mean that only part of the wine came to the altar—perhaps even that the wine for the altar was divided, a part being poured directly onto the sacrifice. Yadin, *I, 410*, accepts Qimron's reading.

35.?-9

The Outer Area for Cult Worship

The outer area for cult worship (perhaps a square 200 × 200 cubits), which was still within the Inner Court, could also be entered by priests, but only when they were about to officiate at worship and when ritually prepared (i.e. in ceremonial attire). The Scroll threatens any who infringe with the death penalty. For biblical references, cf. 1 Kings 8.64f., the restriction in Lev. 21.22f. and the prohibited area 20 cubits wide in Ezek. 41.10 and 43.12f. The demarcation of this area of cult worship together with the demarcation of the priests' area was clearly the subject of vehement debate during the Second Temple period (see below on the Inner Court complex).

35.4

Qimron (*Leshonenu* 42, 144) reads ממנה ('from it').

35.7

According to Milgrom (*JBL* 97, 521), the basis for the severe clothing prescription is not Num. 18.3, but Num. 18.7.

35.10-15

The Peristyle to the West of the Temple Building

See Yadin, I, 161, 182ff. (*I, 207f., 235ff.*), and Milgrom, *JBL* 97,

506ff. A divided peristyle (*parwar*, of free-standing columns on all sides) is to be built behind the Holy of Holies. There, after being carefully separated, the sacrificial animals for the sin- and guilt-offerings of the priests on the one hand, and for the people on the other, are bound. This has scarcely anything to do with the large building to the west in Ezek. 41.12ff. (cf. 46.19), as suggested by Yadin, I, 182 (*I, 235f.*), but rather with the *parbar* to the west, mentioned in 1 Chron. 26.18. Rabbinic tradition knows of a structure with quite a different function in this place (see Yadin, I, 183, [*I, 236*] who, perhaps erroneously, cites the Babylonian Talmud, *Zebaḥim* 55a-b, as a parallel).

In Ezekiel's outline (40.38ff.) a similar division is recognizable: two slaughtering tables stand on the level of the Inner Court, two on the level of the Outer Court—but at the entrance of the north gate. Milgrom (*JBL* 97, 506) translates 35.10ff.: 'You shall fashion a place to the west of the sanctuary and of equal length, a colonnaded stoa for (animals reserved for) purgation- and reparation-offerings so that the purgation-offerings of the priests, the he-goats, the purgation-offerings of the people and their reparation-offerings will be kept apart from each other and one kind will not mix with the other. Indeed, their locations shall be separate from each other in order that the priests shall not err with any of the purgation-offerings of the people or with any of these reparation-offerings for which they will bear grievous sin.' The separation is important because the same sacrifices are laid down both for the priests' offering and for the people's, but the priests may not eat from the sin-offering which was brought for them. In 35.15f., Lev. 22.15f. would therefore be used to this end: 'the priests shall not desecrate the sancta of the Israelites . . . by bringing on themselves a grievous sin when they (the priests) eat their (own) sancta'.

35.15–36.?
Here, too, there were evidently specific instructions for the treatment of the bird-offerings (cf. Lev. 5.8f.).

36.?–38.11

The Inner Court Complex (The Priests' Court)

a. *The Demarcation of the Areas of Holiness*
During the course of the monarchy the opinion must have asserted

itself more and more that in the sanctuary there should be an area accessible exclusively to priests, around the area for cultic worship. Although Solomon in 1 Kings 8.54 still functions as a sort of principal priest, and even later a fixed place was designated for the king in the area for cult worship (2 Chron. 6.13; 2 Kings 11.14, cf. 2 Chron. 23.13; 2 Kings 23.3; cf. also B.-Z. Wacholder, *Eupolemus*, 193f.), Ezekiel's outline (46.1) represents the view that the prince was allowed to approach only as far as the inner threshold of the Inner Court, while the people (probably only the cultically qualified men) had to stop at the entrance to the gate. What is expressed in Ezekiel with particular emphasis against royal cult privilege is also what the Temple Scroll essentially intends: to create around the cult area a clear division between the section for the priests and for the laity, in the form of closed buildings surrounding the court.

The particular *degree* of holiness of the immediate surrounding of the Temple building was scarcely debated in the post-exilic period (cf. above on 35.?-9); the Mishnah, too, is concerned only with distinguishing between the areas for the Israelites, priests and altar (*Middoth* 5.1f.; cf. also *Kelim* 1.9 and cf. Bab. Talmud, *Zebaḥim* 55b-56a). It was the *dimensions* and *nature* of the demarcation of the priests' area on the outside that were under dispute (cf. Lev. 21.22f.). Yadin (I, 145, 154f., 158ff., 185 [*I, 180f., 200f., 204ff., 239f.*]) considers it possible that the Scroll (35.8-9 and 37.9) knows of a wall between the cult area and the outer area for the priests. This would not be at all revolutionary, for here ran what was probably the oldest and hence the innermost line that divided from the outside, i.e. from the area for the laity. According to Hecataeus of Abdera (in Josephus, *Ant.* 1.198f.) a stone wall with two gates surrounded the altar court in the Second Temple. In the early Maccabean period, according to 1 Macc. 9.54, the High Priest Alcimus had 'the wall of the Inner Court of the Sanctuary' removed, whereby he 'tore down the work of the prophets'. These two statements scarcely relate to the limit of the cult area as a whole; their meaning bears upon the division between the areas for the priests and for the laity within the Second Temple's Inner Court which was enclosed with a complex of buildings. There must have been such a demarcation of the so-called 'Men's Court' in the area of the 'Inner Court complex' in the Second Temple with dimensions which varied according to the prevailing bias of the day. Unfortunately, Josephus does not express himself clearly in *Ant.* 13.372f., but he nevertheless assumes for the Solomonic Temple

(*Ant.* 8.95) a dividing wall 3 cubits high which he calls *geision* and which he evidently knew from his own observation (cf. *War* 5.227; *Ant.* 15.419). The Mishnah (*Middoth* 2.6) also assumes such a partition, although marked only with stones. It specifies a depth of 11 cubits for the Men's Court, 11 cubits for the Priests' Court, and lengths for the Men's and Priests' Courts of 135 cubits each—i.e. only on the eastern (short) side of the Inner Court complex measuring 187 × 135. It is also stated in the name of R. Eliezer b. Jacob that the Men's Court lay three steps lower by a total of 3.5 cubits (the Woman's Court lay lower still by the same amount). This division must also have been controversial during the Second Temple period. It apparently consisted, for a while, of a proper wall which Alcimus had torn down to make less obvious the exclusion of the laity. In their architectural outlines, Ezekiel and the Scroll represent the ideal according to extreme priestly opinion: the area for the priests and the area for the laity are arranged as separate complexes of court buildings. Moreover, the Scroll follows the idea of concentric holiness so consistently that the whole structure has been shaped in the same way to all four points of the compass. In addition, it arranges the areas for the laity (the 'Middle' and 'Outer' Courts, see below) according to the needs of the twelve tribes.

b. *Dimensions*
As was shown in the introduction to columns 3–48, the Inner Court consists of an enclosing structure around an area of 280 × 280 cubits. Externally, each side of the court consists of:

> a 40 cubit gateway in the centre;
> a 120 (3 × 40) cubit section of wall to the right of the gateway;
> a 120-cubit section of wall to the left of the gateway;
> a 280 × 280 (7 × 40) length of enclosing building (or accessible court surface).

According to Yadin these data defined an area enclosed by a wall 7 cubits thick (an assumed figure), giving dimensions of 294 × 294 cubits for the outside of the wall. But the figure of 280 cubits for the length is better applied to the length of the enclosing buildings (the portico) and therefore tells us nothing about the external dimensions of the court. These dimensions depend on the depth of the enclosing structure (and thus on the size of the presumed corner buildings). In the two outer courts, the information supplied about the gatehouses offers some assistance. Here in the Inner Court, according to the data provided, the gatehouses have a ground plan of 40 × 40, their walls are 7 cubits thick, and the space inside (from [inner] corner to [inner] corner) is 26 cubits long. Unfortunately, the figure for the external height has not been preserved. In the gatehouse, the opening is 14 cubits wide and 28 cubits high and above it there are 14 cubits of 'timberwork', as is the case in all the gatehouses of the whole Temple structure. Unfortunately, the information as to how far the gatehouse projected beyond the wall on the inside and on the outside is missing from the preserved text. The outer dimensions and the width of the ancillary buildings cannot be determined from the surviving data. Nevertheless, certain calculations are possible from the reconstruction of the Middle and Outer Courts, since the figure for the depth of the Middle Court (100 cubits) has been supplied (see below). Presumably the Inner Court had no closed ancillary building. 37.9 speaks of (1) an 'inner porch' on the outer wall of the Inner Court and col. 37.6 of (2) a 'lower porch' in which cooking sites are to be installed at the gateways. Since the 'lower porch' (see *ad loc.*) can also be called the 'outer porch' (when seen from the wall of the court), a sort of two-tiered stoa should be considered. But it is not necessary to accept this interpretation if one assumes a double ancillary building.

A comparison with Ezek. 42 leads to the conclusion given. Possibly a wall should be added between the two porches, an 'inner wall of the Inner Court' (see below) which did not mark off the area for cult worship but merely separated the dining recesses from a porch that was otherwise entirely open to the interior of the court. In Ezekiel the structure is complicated: 3 stories, each with a frontage that was set back somewhat, because the 'galleries' that extended along the interior and the exterior were not thought of as pillared constructions (as was the case in the two outer courts). But these 'cell constructions' of Ezekiel's form only a part of the boundary of the north and south sides of the Inner Court as well as the long sides of the Temple building. These cells at the north open northwards to the gallery and to the passage (to the court wall). The Scroll proceeds quite consistently, according to the quadratic ideal, towards a completely symmetrical four-sided portico. The dimensions of the gateway in the Scroll would also permit a three-storeyed construction. But in such a case a thickness of 7 cubits (according to Yadin, by analogy with the gatehouse) or 6 cubits (as Ezekiel) would be appropriate. As in Ezekiel, other functionally determined architectural elements were probably also defined more precisely in the Scroll (e.g. sections for the priests in the inner and outer cultic areas).

Yadin's assumption of a thickness of 7 cubits for the court wall relies on the thickness of the gatehouse wall. But since in the Middle Court, as in the Outer Court, the heights of the walls amount to seven times their respective thickness, Yadin would apparently require a height of 49 cubits here. Such a structure would be somewhat precarious architecturally, unless one assumes, as Yadin does, porches of at least two stories. But possibly a wall only 3 cubits thick and 21 cubits high was intended. In Ezek. 40.5 the boundary wall has a width of 6 cubits, though admittedly the gatehouses there (40.6ff.) do not have a square ground plan but measure 50 cubits deep and 25 cubits wide. Moreover, the gateway contains a portico with a depth of 8 cubits plus pillars 2 cubits thick on the side adjacent to the Outer Court. Then comes a gate opening 10 cubits wide and a gateway 13 cubits wide. On each side, within this part of the gatehouse, there were three recesses with a width of 6 cubits, divided by pillars 5 cubits wide. The author of the Scroll conforms this gatehouse to the quadratic ideal of 40 × 40. Yadin finds this figure strange but in fact it is provided, in a way, by Ezekiel: the depth of his gatehouse is 40 cubits without a porch, while in the Scroll the proportions of the court areas are 7 : 12 : 40 × 40. It is also noteworthy that in Ezekiel the length of the second court, which was 7 steps lower, is given as 100 cubits from gate frontage to gate frontage, but the gatehouse of the second court is just as deep as the ancillary buildings (including the wall of the court, Ezek. 40.17f.). That is to say, Ezekiel did not know of any projection from the gatehouse into the open space of the court, and understood the court depth of 100 cubits as the depth of the unbuilt court surface (in its strict sense). If the Scroll falls into line with this particular instance, then important conclusions emerge; but these may only be drawn in the light of the reconstruction as a whole. It is therefore advisable to read first the notes on the two outer courts—the Middle Court especially, but also the Outer Court, because it is for the latter that most data have been preserved.

This much is at any rate clear: whereas Ezekiel encloses directly in front of the Temple only an area of 100 × 100 cubits with *three* sides containing *three* gatehouses to form a square inner court surface, the Scroll's outline calls for construction around the *whole* of it. This difference requires considerable elaboration. Ezekiel's construction of the inner architectural complex is a rectangle with external dimensions of 200 (east and west sides) × 350 (or 340) set right up against the west side of the outer court or 10 cubits away from it. It practically cuts off the inside of the area for cult worship (hence the cumbersome approach to the priests' cells by a corridor on the outside). Corresponding to this arrangement, the Scroll clearly stipulates an area for cult worship of 200 × 200 cubits, and surrounds it with a portico complex of 280 cubits (inside length). Furthermore, in the Outer Court it assumes a definite projection of the gatehouse on the outside, and presumably the same with the Middle and Inner Courts (remnants of the text, but without figures, are extant). The uncertainty lies in whether, and how far, the gatehouses were also supposed to project into the open courtyard.

36.4

Yadin (II, 108 [*II, 153*]) restores the beginning of the line '[to the cor]ner of the gate(?) [120 cubits and] the gate width 40 . . . ' In his opinion this refers to the inner corners of the gatehouse which are to measure 120 cubits from the '(inner) corner', i.e. without the thickness of the wall. On this, see above. If the phrase 'to the corner of the gatehouse' is taken in its strict sense and if 'corner' is understood to apply to the gatehouse, it could be concluded that the gatehouse did not project into the open court. But the 'corner of the gatehouse' could equally well mean the 'corner *at* the gatehouse'. If so, the 'corner' does not have to be that of the gatehouse itself.

36.7-8

Yadin (II, 109 [*II, 154*]) thinks this might imply that not all of the four gates allowed access, perhaps specifically not the east gate, as is the case in Ezek. 44.1. But this can only be so if the measurements given here for the passage through the gateway do not apply to the east gate. Since particular measurements are not provided in the case of the Outer or Middle Courts either for the eastern gates or even for the middle gate on the eastern side, this assumption would be equally incorrect here. What we have is simply a re-phrasing, for the sake of clarity, of the fact that the subject has shifted from the *external* dimensions of the gatehouse to the passage through the gateway and thus to the *interior* dimension. An investigation of the functional division of the gatehouses is thus entirely justified; cf. below on 37.?-5.

37.?-5

Here details about the porticoes (*parwar*) within the walls have unfortunately been lost. Lines 4–5 probably describe the method laid down for the supply and—after sacrificing—the distribution of the people's offering. It may have been intended to transfer the offering inside the gatehouse, insofar as it lies outside the boundary of the court (300 × 300?). If the gatehouse is divided exactly in half by the court boundary (cf. Mishnah, *Middoth*, for a similar bisection of the enclosing structures) there would still be a width of 20 cubits (outer measurement only 13) available within the gatehouse. If the sacrifice was not slaughtered in the Inner Court (cf. Lev. 7.29ff.) then this would apply only to the transfer of the parts prescribed for burning on the altar and to those assigned to the priests. This is probably a specific example of the Scroll's constant attempt to distinguish between offerings for the people and for the priests.

37.5
According to Milgrom (*JBL* 97, 521f.) this concerns the priests' portions of the *shelamim*-offerings (Lev. 7.29-34) which, as lines 11–14 pointedly require, has to be eaten in the Priests' Court, separately from the sacrificial meal of the laity in the Outer Court (21.e-3).

37.9
Qimron (*Leshonenu* 42, 144) reads אצל קיר החצר החיצון.

37.10-14
Cf. Milgrom, *JQR* 71, 91ff.; *JBL* 97, 512f. The architectural layout is not transparent. Does 'lower *parwar*' in line 6 mean that at least one upper storey is to be put in the structure enclosing the court? But cf. Ezek. 40.18f. Furthermore, the expression 'wall of the Outer Court' in line 9 might mean 'outer wall of the court', and hence an inner wall delimiting the altar area might need to be assumed (cf. Yadin *ad loc.*).

37.13f.
This passage provides kitchens in the corners of the court for the priests' offerings which are to be strictly separated from the people's sacrifices (lines 11f.). Similarly, but not in all corners, Ezek. 46.23 arranges such kitchens in the Men's Court. Here, in the Scroll, these would be set in the Middle Court. The corner buildings (which are to be assumed, against Yadin's original assumptions) are probably to be connected with such cooking installations.

38.?-11

These lines have unfortunately suffered considerable damage and, despite additional fragments from the Rockefeller Museum, they can only be partly reconstructed. They contain further details about the application of the design of the court and clearly concern especially the first-fruits and their festivals.

38.8

Reading הבאה (instead of היאה) with Qimron, *IEJ* 28, 165.

38.9ff.

The readings and restorations adopted here follow Qimron (*Leshonenu* 42, 144): (9) . . . ולימ[ין ה]שער הזה כול המנחה . . . חטאת אשר
. . . שמה ייהיו אוכלים . . . העוף ולתורים ולבני היונה . . . (10)

These are now accepted by Yadin, *II, 163*. On line 10 see also Milgrom, *JQR* 71, 93. On line 15 see Qimron, *IEJ* 28, 165, who reads בחוץ, corrected from מחוץ (?).

38.12–40.4

The Middle Court (Court for cultically qualified men)

The following data are preserved:

(a) 100 cubits court depth (38.12), i.e. from 150 to 250 cubits (or 140 to 240, using inner measurements) in all four directions
(b) 480 cubits length (38.13f.)
(c) 4 cubits thickness of court wall
(d) 28 cubits (= 7×4 cubits thickness of wall) height of court wall (38.14f.)
(e) 3.5 cubits distance between 'recesses' on the outside of the court wall (38.15f.)
(f) 3 gatehouses on each side of the court (39.11ff.)
(g) 99 cubits each section of wall between gates and between gates and corners (39.13ff.)
(h) 28×28 cubits outer dimensions of gatehouse (39.16).

Further to (a): The court depth of 100 cubit could be measured

(1) as an overall measurement from the outer wall of the Inner Court to the outer wall of the Middle Court, including the thickness of the latter wall (4 cubits).

(2)   as the distance from the outside of the wall of the Inner Court to the inside of the wall of the Middle Court, excluding the thickness of 4 cubits for the latter wall.

(3)   as the depth of the built-up area of the court which was not closed (and hence accessible to pedestrians), and thus including the floor of the portico.

(4)   as the depth of the enclosed court surface within the porticoes.

In Ezekiel (see above on the Inner Court) the depth of the court is measured as 100 cubits from gate front to gate front (= overall frontage of the ancillary buildings) and hence as the depth of the open court surface (Ezek. 40.19).

Further to (b): Putting together the information of (g)-(h), we arrive at the following:

3 gate widths (3 × 28)	84
4 sections of wall (4 × 99)	396
Total length	480

The distance from the centre of one gatehouse to the centre of the next is thus 127 cubits (99 + 14 + 14). Four such sections produce a total length of 508 cubits, in which a building with a size of 14 cubits (half the width of a gatehouse) is to be set in each corner. This 508 × 508 square would be an idealized symmetrical measurement divisible into 16 squares of 127 × 127 cubits. Without the thickness of the wall—i.e. the inside depth up to the court wall—it would be 500 × 500—the square of the 'Outer Court' in Ezekiel (Ezek. 42.15ff.; 45.2—inside measurement), and thus a traditional size. In early Judaism this had a real significance: the Mishnah (*Middoth* 2.1) also attests it as the length of the balustrade surrounding the Holy Enclosure and keeping out aliens and the unclean in the Herodian Temple. In the Scroll's plan this function is fulfilled by the enclosure of the Outer Court (see below).

Further to (a) and (b): According to Yadin, 480 × 480 are the outside dimensions. Since he takes 280 × 280 as the area within the walls and 294 × 294 as the external dimensions, it is impossible to obtain a court depth of exactly 100 cubits.

When measured within the area of the 500 × 500 square a court depth of 100 cubits would provide a square 300 × 300 cubits as the outer size of the Inner Court—an excellent result from the point of view of architectural appearance and function. Alternatively, following Ezekiel, one would have to calculate the open built-up area of the court from the 480 × 480 square, and accept outer dimensions of 280 × 280 for the Inner Court. This is possible, but in this case not only would the proportions in the Inner Court be narrower, but also an inconsistency would arise in the computing of the data: namely, for the Inner Court 280 × 280 are *external* dimensions, while for the Middle Court 480 × 480 is the sum of the widths of the gatehouses and the sections of wall provided with ancillary buildings, and likewise for the Outer Court with 1590 × 1590 or 'about 1600 × 1600' cubits.

The depth of the ancillary buildings is, of course, indicated by the 480 × 480 square, but one might also imagine a portico supported by columns or pillars as an additional part of the accessible court area. The depth of the gateways (28 cubits) also provides clues. If the gatehouse projected the equivalent of one wall thickness on the outside, as is the case in the Outer Court, then from the inside of the wall there would be a space of 20 cubits in the court, of which 10 cubits is the distance to the 480 × 480 square. We should note the difference between the dimensions of the gatehouse in the Scroll and those in Ezekiel. This difference is partly determined by the fact that the Scroll places twelve gates on four sides, but partly also because of the desired sizes of the court—an ideal size of 508 (externally) and a traditional size 500 (the inside of the walls). In the corners of the court one might well assume, by analogy with Ezek. 46.21-24, kitchens for the laymen's sacrifices, probably connected directly to the corner buildings.

From the outside, the impression made by such a square complex of buildings with three gates on each side and a wall arranged with supporting columns (possibly with projecting corner buildings) makes one think of a fortress. In fact, in the vicinity of Palestine—in Egypt—a square construction of this sort was used for frontier fortresses on the east of the delta (cf. E. Oren, '"Migdol"—Fortresses in North-Western Sinai', *Qadmoniot*, 10, 71-6). Furthermore, such a construction had projections from its wall, and powerful ones at that. The author of the Scroll was perhaps as familiar with this kind of building as with Near Eastern, and particularly Hellenistic, buildings on a large scale, such as agoras and temples.

Yadin (I, 186ff.; cf. also 147 [*I, 241ff.; cf. 190f.*]) feels that this Middle Court is an entirely new creation on the part of the Scroll.

But this view holds true only when the court is seen *architecturally* in a certain sense, since, in the First and Second Temples, the section that was open to cultically qualified men was not divided off by such a court enclosure, but simply marked out with the Inner Temple Court (see above, and cf. also Josephus, *War* 5.194ff.). But from the point of view of *function* this court is in no way an innovation; it constitutes that area of holiness which women were not permitted to enter and which lies in front of the area that was only accessible to priests. The Scroll is quite consistent when it makes a clear architectural separation of this area of holiness. Furthermore, Ezekiel's 'Outer Court' is perhaps also regarded as a court for cultically qualified men only. In this respect is the Temple Scroll being more conciliatory when it adds the third court on analogy with the actual Temple's 'Women's Court'?

38.12

According to Qimron (*Leshonenu* 42, 144; *IEJ* 28, 165) we should read ועשיתה [ח]צר שנית סובבת את החצר הפנימית רחוב מאה באמה.

38.15

What is intended by the תאים which were to be set at intervals of 3.5 cubits outside on the court wall? Yadin (I, 188f. [*I, 243f.*]) thinks of a closed type of construction added on the outside, which would nonetheless be accessible from the inside. And yet in 40.10f. where the same thing (but without any dimensions being given) is specified for the outer side of the Outer Court, Yadin interprets differently. Furthermore, it is stated there that these *tā'îm* extended from the base to the top of the wall (49 cubits high!). Now, this is more suitable for a wall construction of regularly spaced projections or buttresses, which were quite common in oriental and Egyptian building traditions and were known, though at times reduced to pilasters, in Hellenistic architecture. One of the most recent reconstructions of the Herodian enclosures in the Temple shows such wall constructions (*Qadmoniot* 5, 79f.). Possibly these buttresses are thought of as extensions of the partition walls within the ancillary buildings. Thus in the Middle Court one would assume, for example, eight partition walls and buttresses (with nine at the corner) per section of wall (with 99 cubits there are few choices for division). If the corner building projected at least the same amount, the ninth buttress might be higher.

39.4-10

According to the text remaining in these lines, the following could
not enter the Middle Court:

(1) Proselytes and their descendants until the fourth generation
     (line 5). For the Outer Court, cf. 40.6 (until the third
     generation). Yadin (I, 191f. [*I, 247f.*]) derives this from Gen.
     15.16 and draws attention to 4Q174 (4QFlorilegium); *DJD*,
     V, 53) 1.3. On this also G. Blidstein, *RQ* 8, 431-35; J.M.
     Baumgarten, *Studies in Qumran Law*, 75ff.
(2) Women.
(3) Children up to 20 years old (see line 11).
(4) All men (over 20) who have not paid the Temple tax (half
     shekel).

39.8

Restoring, with Qimron, ‏[פריו]ן נפשו‎ (*Leshonenu* 42, 144) and ‏ישלים חוק‎
at the beginning of the line (*IEJ* 28, 166).

39.10

Restoring, with Qimron, ‏ישאו ממנו את מחצית הש[ק]ל‎ (*Leshonenu* 42,
144).

39.11–40.?

Here are given the names and sequence of the gatehouses and the
distances between them. Like the Outer Court (see below), the
Middle Court has three gatehouses on each side, named after the
sons of Jacob (tribes of Israel). The count begins at the northern gate
on the east side with Simeon; the middle gate is named after Levi, the
southern one after Judah, then the text breaks off. With the aid of
40.13ff. (see below) the rest of the sequence can be reconstructed. For
the order of the tribes cf. also above 23.?-25.2 (the Wood Festival).

39.14

'of Simeon' (above the line?) is questionable (Qimron, *IEJ* 28, 166).

40.?-5

This seems to contain a prohibition against coming in priestly garb
from the Inner Court to the Middle Court (cf. Ezek. 42.14; 44.17-19).
The Scroll may also have been acquainted with other special

ceremonial clothing which was taken off and put on in the housing for the laver (32.10ff.; 33.1-7). The basis for this prescription is Lev. 6.2ff.

40.5–45.6

The Outer Court (Court for the Israelites); see Figs. 1-4, pp. 144-47

The following data are preserved:

(a) ? cubits, depth of court (the number clearly began with ש) (40.7).
(b) 1600 cubits (כ = about?), length of sides (40.8f.)
(c) 7 cubits, thickness of wall
(d) 49 cubits (7 × wall thickness) cubits, height of wall (40.9f.)
(e) *tā'îm* on the outside of the wall from the base to the top of the wall (40.10f.)
(f) 3 gatehouses per side, 50 × 50 ground plan and 70 cubits high (40.11-13)
(g) 360 cubits, section of wall between gatehouses or between gatehouses and corners (40.13ff.). With this, 1590 cubits (3 × 50 width of gatehouse + 4 × 360 section of wall) is indirectly given as the length of the side of the court.
(h) 7 cubits, projection of gatehouse beyond the court wall on the outside (41.12)
(i) 36 cubits, projection of gatehouse from the inside of the court wall into the court area (41.13)
(j) 14 cubits, width of gate opening 28 cubits height of gate opening (41.14f.)
(k) ancillary structures inside on the 360 cubits sections of wall:

    1 back room (*ḥeder*) or chamber
       10 cubits deep
       20 cubits long
       14 cubits high
       2 cubits, thickness of partition wall
    2 front room (*niškâ*) or cell
       10 cubits deep
       20 cubits long
       2 cubits, thickness of wall
       14 cubits high
       3 cubits, width of door (42.1-3)

    3   gallery-portico (*parwar*)
        10 cubits deep (42.4)
        18 room units (front + back room) with gallery-
        portico (42.4-6)
    4   staircase in the gallery-portico against the gatehouse;
        in the second and third stories, the same
        division of rooms (42.8ff.), making 3 × 18
        = 54 room units (front + back room) per
        section of 360 cubits (44.3-10)
    5   52 room units set in the section at the corner (44.12)
    6   On the roof above the third storey, columns fitted
        with planks set up for the erection of the tabernacles
        (42.10ff.).

(l)   Round about (in front of the gate openings?) a terrace of 14
      cubits, with 12 steps up to the terrace in front of the gates
      (46.5-8).
(m)   100 cubits, embankment (*ḥyl*) (46.9)

Unresolved questions

(a) The specification 'about/approximately (כ) 1600 cubits' in
40.8f. (see above 1(b)) is strange. Of course this preposition does not
necessarily have to be interpreted as 'about/approximately'; the exact
length of the court might also have been intended. But perhaps the
author was aware that, circumstances permitting, the corner of the
peristyle could be formed so that the corners of the 1600 × 1600
square overlapped the corners of the corner building to some extent,
if the minimal solution is taken up. With the maximal solution, it is
possible that the columns of the peristyle corner were so formed that
they jut into the court area of 1600 × 1600 cubits, filling the corner of
the court and, depending on the thickness of the columns, producing
there a length which was only 'about' 1600 cubits. Unfortunately, the
outline, such as has been preserved, contains no specifications which
would permit an unequivocal and precise calculation of the court or
of the corners of the peristyle and the buildings.

(b) A four-sided portico ran around the court, but with or without
some kind of corner buildings? In the case of a Temple design, corner
buildings may be assumed with reasonable certainty. In the Orient,
tower-like corner structures with a specific relationship to the
gatehouse were quite common in such designs and, like the latter,

they sometimes projected beyond the line of the wall. One may therefore assume such structures which probably contained kitchens, as is also the case in the Priests' Court (cf. also Ezek. 46.23). Possibly they were intended to be as tall as the gatehouses: this would have a practical value in view of the flues for the smoke from the kitchens. Perhaps on the outside the division of the wall into sections by means of pilasters was also continued on the corner buildings. The cooking installations would be accessible through the corner of the peristyle on the ground floor, with some further arrangement in the upper stories being necessary. Perhaps, too, the particular detail that only fifty-two instead of fifty-four room units are set at each corner (44.12) is related to the cooking installations: the animals slaughtered for sacrifice could certainly not have been prepared for cooking in the slaughtering site in the Inner Court.

(c) The precise division of the 360-cubit stoas into 18 room units remains uncertain. For the depth of the ancillary buildings within the 360-cubit sections of wall, the specifications (see above 1(k)) of a back room of 10 cubits, a front room of 10 cubits and 10 cubits of stoa, have been completely preserved. So has the thickness of 2 cubits for the longitudinal partition wall, but without indicating whether the thickness of the partition wall is intended to be inclusive or exclusive, and thus whether the overall depth was 30 or 36 cubits. Two basic alternative reconstructions are consequently given, A with inclusive dimensions and B with exclusive dimensions. In reconstruction A the 50 × 50 gatehouse which extends 7 cubits beyond the court wall on the outside, would have had to project 6 cubits beyond the depth of the ancillary buildings into the court area. In reconstruction B the frontage of the peristyle and the frontage of the gatehouse are in alignment.

(d) While the thickness of the longitudinal partition wall is given (2 cubits), no figure exists for the thickness of the partition walls that ran perpendicular to the court wall and of which there were seventeen per 360 cubit section, forming eighteen room units of 20 cubits. This 20 cubits without doubt includes the thickness of the longitudinal partition wall. But how are these partition walls to be placed? One could start immediately from one side with the entire thickness of one partition wall and thus reach a comparatively simple uniform division, as far as the sections at the corners are concerned. However, between two gatehouses one would have to divide the thickness of the partition wall between the 20 cubit lines in order to reach a uniform division. Since the steps at the tower structure up to the upper stories still have to be incorporated, there is a further complication. It would be natural to use the 5 cubits' thickness of the partition wall in the extension towards the court for the pillars which were to be placed in the corners of the peristyle (assuming a pillar of 5 × 5 cubits). It is uncertain whether square pillars or round columns were used for the stoa complex and galleries. Because of the physical problems involved in supporting such a substantial three-storeyed complex, pillars would be more suitable—under certain circumstances, even pillars measuring 5 × 5 cubits might be appropriate in the 5 cubits' extension of the partition walls. These would be perpendicular to the main wall, extending beyond it into buttresses and pilasters (depending on thickness, to a maximum of 7 cubits corresponding to the projection of the gatehouse). Outside on sections of court wall and on the gatehouse walls, these formed *tā'îm* (see above 1(e)) between the base and the mural crown. In the court structure, this arrangement would produce seventeen pillars per 360-cubit section of ancillary construction, with four pillars in the corners of the peristyle, making a total of 276. But one could also take double this number of narrower pillars or columns, in which case the doorways of each of the eighteen room units provide the pattern for the layout, and at every second pillar (column) the perspective leads to a doorway. In this case, the peristyle corner has several possible shapes.

(e) It is not clear how far the base of the court wall rose above ground level on the outside, nor how substantial the height of the mural crown should be and how far it was to overhang. If we subtract from the given height of the wall—49 cubits—the height of the ancillary buildings on the inside (14 + 14 + 14 = 42 cubits), then 7 cubits remain. Should the thickness of the ceiling also be subtracted?

(f) With the known archaeological examples in mind, we should assume that the peristyle in the court lay somewhat above the level of the court surface, perhaps at the level of the base of the wall on the outside.

(g) According to 46.5ff. a terrace 14 cubits deep is to be set (only?) in the front of the gatehouses. Twelve steps lead up to it in front of the gatehouses. Beyond that is an embankment 100 cubits deep (what was its gradient?) to separate the Temple from the city.

(h) Unfortunately there is no way to determine the length of the cubit used: the possibilities extend from the shortest Herodian cubit of 32.25 cm, through the 'Attic cubit' of 46.20 cm, to the 'great cubit' of 52.25 cm (under certain circumstances even 56 cm). When one considers the structural problems of rooms with a ceiling span of 20 × 10 cubits (in such large numbers!) one is inclined to favour the shorter cubit.

The Maximal Solution

From the sum of the gatehouse widths (3 × 50 = 150) and the sections of wall with ancillary buildings on the inside (4 × 360 = 1440), i.e. 1590 cubits, 5 cubits are missing from each side to make up the court length of 1600 cubits given in 40.8f. This discrepancy is best explained by a lateral closing wall 5 cubits thick. This could also be the (maximal) thickness of the partition walls of the ancillary buildings and possibly also of the pillars in the peristyle. Assuming this explanation of the two figures of 1590 and 1600, two reconstructions (A and B) emerge, each with three variations:

A.   Assuming that the thickness of the partition wall (2 cubits) is *included* in the area of the front room, back room and stoa section, each of which are 10 cubits deep, the overall depth of the ancillary buildings from the court wall to the 1600 × 1600 court surface is 30 cubits. Hence the gatehouses project 6 cubits into the court itself. (This detail is not provided, unlike the specification of a gate projection of 7 cubits beyond the line of the wall on the outside.) In this case, there are three ways of connecting the 5 × 5 square between the corners of the 1590 × 1590 square and the 1600 × 1600 square with the sections of the portico.

Variation A1 has the 1590-cubit line run 795 cubits from the middle of the structure along the portico frontage so that the 1600 x 1600 square extends back into the stoa (even by as much as the thickness of a pillar) making an architecturally meaningful division of the stoa into units which correspond to the room units composed of front and back rooms. Such powerful proportions would suit the huge building.

Variation A2 takes the 1600 cubit line 3 cubits to the inside in the direction of the court.

Variation A3 moves it a further 2 cubits up to the edge of the court surface.

B.   The same three variations are also available in reconstruction B, where *exclusive* dimensions are intended, namely 10 cubits, depth of backroom; 2 cubits partition wall; 10 cubits, depth of frontroom; 2 cubits, partition wall at stoa; 10 cubits, depth of stoa; 2 cubits, thickness of parapet on the court side (this does not apply on the ground floor), and perhaps also the thickness of the pillars, provided they were not 5 cubits thick as in the closures of the sides.

The following diagram and the tables elucidate these possibilities. The most likely in each case is variation 3. The maximal variant B3 has the advantage of offering satisfactory exterior dimensions to a visually plausible solution both for the side of the court and for an exact definition of 1600 × 1600 square. The entire structure of the sanctuary, including the gatehouse projections on the outside, measures 1700 × 1700 cubits, making a distance of 850 cubits from the centre of the sanctuary. If we subtract 250 cubits (reckoning that the Middle Court measures 500 × 500 cubits on the outside) from this figure, the overall depth of the Outer Court, including wall and gatehouses, is 600 cubits (cf. 40.7?). The exterior division of the frontage of the building is also plausible: with corner buildings of 48 cubits (or, if they are intended to project 7 cubits like the gates, 55 cubits) to left and right on the outside and the three gatehouses with a width of 50 cubits, an almost completely uniform frame for the four portico complexes, each of 360 cubits, is ensured. It would be completely uniform if the buttresses or pilasters, which according to 40.10f. (see 1(e)) divide the wall into *tā'îm* on the outside, were 2 cubits wide, so that these pilasters went round the corner. In this case, dimensions of 50 × 50 cubits could also be obtained for the corner buildings, without the projection of 7 cubits.

VARIATIONS OF A = INCLUSIVE DEPTH OF ANCILLARY BUILDINGS (30 cubits)

B = EXCLUSIVE DEPTH (36 cubits)

	Court surface within the wall	Outer circuit of wall	Perimeter of construction with gatehouse projection of 7 cubits
A1	1650 × 1650	1664 × 1664	1678 × 1678
A2	1656 × 1656	1670 × 1670	1684 × 1684
A3	1660 × 1660	1674 × 1674	1688 × 1688

B1	1662 × 1662	1676 × 1676	1690 × 1690
B2	1668 × 1668	1682 × 1682	1696 × 1696
B3	1672 × 1672	1686 × 1686	1700 × 1700

The Minimal Solution

The 1600 × 1600 square can also be construed as the court surface *including* the space within the peristyle (depth of the stoa). Taking inclusive dimensions (reconstruction A) this produces:

Unbuilt court surface	1580 × 1580
(1590 × 1590 including half the depth of the stoa)	
Surface within the court wall	1640 × 1600
Outer circuit of court wall	1654 × 1654
Perimeter of construction with gatehouse projection	1668 × 1668
Perimeter of construction including terrace	1696 × 1696
Perimeter of construction including embankment	1896 × 1896

The advantage of this reconstruction is the simple formation of the peristyle corner, although admittedly the corner pillar of the court (hypothetically 5 × 5, half the depth of the stoa) would not lie on the extension of the 5 cubit wall that closed off the sides, unless this were included as the first partition wall in the first room unit. Up to the gatehouse this reconstruction would make a clear and simple division possible, but between the gatehouses it would appear quite differently. The corners of the 1600 × 1600 square would project into the corner space and yet still belong to the court area (including the space within the peristyle). Perhaps a consideration such as this—the partial architectural overlapping of court and corner space—is the reason for the expression 'about 1600 cubits'.

Taking exclusive dimension (reconstruction B) the following dimensions emerge:

Unbuilt court surface	1576 × 1576
Surface within the court wall	1648 × 1648
Outer circuit of court wall	1662 × 1662
Perimeter of court construction with gatehouse projection	1676 × 1676
Perimeter of construction including terrace	1704 × 1704
Perimeter of constructon including embankment	1904 × 1904

See Figure 2 (p. 145) for a sketch of the minimal solution.

Between Utopia and Practicality

This huge Outer Court, which by far exceeds the Herodian construction, especially in its east-west line, corresponds functionally to that part of the Herodian temple which was also accessible to women (hence called the Women's Forecourt). The striking enlargement of this court implies that the contemporary Temple was believed to have been built with completely inadequate dimensions. In view of the population increase during the Second Temple, and the fact that since the Exile only the Jerusalem Temple was to be exclusively available to all Jews, this implied criticism is quite understandable. At the time of Christ, visiting the Temple at the festivals took on such proportions that ritually correct procedure, at least according to the strict Essene tradition, was no longer guaranteed. When, for example, the Scroll stipulates that the Passover lambs should be eaten in the Temple courts (see above), then even this huge construction seems modest.

40.5-6
The Outer Court is also accessible to (ritually pure) Israelite women and children and furthermore to (descendants of) proselytes in the third generation. When compared to the Herodian Temple this Outer Court corresponds in function to the 'Women's Forecourt' which had thus architecturally replaced the 'Gentile Forecourt'.

40.7
Yadin's first suggested restoration (II, 246; supported by Qimron, *Leshonenu* 42, 145) 's[ix hundred cubits]' is far too great in the light of his assumption of an external size of 1590 × 1590; it should be 555 (including a wall thickness of 7 cubits). With a Middle Court of 480 × 480 (Yadin), a court depth of 600 cubits would certainly produce an outside length of 1680 cubits but with a Middle Court of 500 × 500, an outside length of 1700. However, Yadin (*I, 245f.*) arrives *de facto* at 500 × 500, although he puts down 1590 × 1590 for the Outer Court (*I, 414f.*). His new suggested restoration at 40.7 (cf. *II, 170*) of 560 cubits also conflicts with his reconstruction (see above).

40.8
'About (כ) 1600 cubits': the reading is somewhat uncertain. On this matter see above. It does not need to be an approximate figure.

40.9f.

The height of the wall (49 cubits) is seven times its thickness.

40.10

We follow the improved reading of Qimron (*Leshonenu* 42, 145)
ותאים עשוים בו ולשעריו. This would also give a section of wall framed
by pilasters on the gatehouse to left and right of the entrance. A
prominent example of such an external form can be found at
Palmyra and, more especially, in the reconstruction drawn up for the
Herodian (!) Temple by B. Lalor in *Qadmoniot* 5, 78f. Yadin (*I, 405*)
holds to his original reading and interpretation. But the precise
description ('from the base to the mural crown') shows that these are
scarcely cells (closed spaces) added on.

40.13–41.20

The Gates with their Sections of Wall

The author of the Scroll regards the gatehouses with their attached
wall sections and ancillary buildings as an architectural unit, as a
portico structure, or wing, of the court. The names of the gates and
their sequence, which were obviously the same as in the Middle
Court, recall the order of the tribes at the Wood Festival (23.?–25.2).
Yadin (II, 121f. [*II, 171f.*]) reconstructs the complete allocation of
gates with the aid of the Rockefeller Museum fragment 43.366
(incorporated in the translation in ° °) thus:

Gates on the east side	(1) in the north:	Simeon
	(2) in the centre:	Levi
	(3) in the south:	Judah
Gates on the south side	(1) in the east:	Reuben
	(2) in the centre:	Joseph
	(3) in the west:	Benjamin
Gates on the west side	(1) in the south:	Issachar
	(2) in the centre:	Zebulun
	(3) in the north:	Dan
Gates on the north side	(1) in the west:	Gad
	(2) in the centre:	Naphtali
	(3) in the east:	Asher

The simple sequence, taken clockwise and beginning with Simeon,
certainly does not imply order of rank, for clearly Levi, at the middle

gate in the east, should take priority. Yadin (I, 102) has compared the order of the tribes with those in Pseudo-Philo, *Liber Antiquitatum Biblicarum*, Ezek. 48.30ff. (city gates!), Ezek. 48.1-29 (tribal portions in the Holy Land), Dt. 27.12-13, Num. 2 (arrangement of camps) and Rev. 7.5-8. The correspondence between the sequence of the tribes at the Wood Festival (cols. 23ff.) and Pseudo-Philo is striking:

Levi	Judah
Joseph	Benjamin
	(or vice versa)
Reuben	Simeon
Issachar	Zebulun
Gad	Asher
Dan	Naphtali

As was remarked above on the Wood Festival, this series corresponds essentially to the order of rank (but not sequence) of the names of the gates when one compares the paired tribes. The series of gate names in Ezek. 48.30ff. also contains these pairs in a slightly altered order; they are also found in Dt. 27 with slight changes. The relationship with Num. 2 is more complicated. Here too, Issachar and Zebulun, Joseph (Ephraim and Manasseh) and Benjamin, Dan and Asher are adjacent to one another, but with Gad and Asher, Dan and Naphtali separated. On the other hand, the only corresponding group of three that is found here is Dan, Asher and Naphtali in the north, so that Num. 2 was certainly not seen by the author of the Scroll as a model for the series of gates. In addition to Yadin's examples of tribal sequences, one should compare Num. 1.5ff., 20ff., and obviously Gen. 49, where apart from the 'chiastic' order for Dan–Gad–Asher–Naphtali, the same pairs are found, though admittedly in a different order.

It thus appears that we have in the Scroll a combination of traditionally paired tribes with an order of rank which, according to a priestly point of view, begins with Levi. The order of importance of the gate descriptions would thus be: 1. Levi (middle gate), 2. Judah, 3. Simeon, 4. Joseph, 5. Benjamin, 6. Reuben, 7. Zebulun, 8. Issachar, 9. Gad, 10. Naphtali, 11. Dan, 12. Asher. This assumes that the middle gate always indicates priority. If otherwise, we proceed: 1. Levi, 2. Judah, 3. Simeon and thereafter clockwise.

This sequence of the tribes at the gates is also used for allotting the room units in the ancillary buildings—see below on 44.3ff.

41.16

אֲרַשְׁכִים, 'posts', is a new word and obviously (Yadin, *ad loc.*) a Persian loanword.

42.7-9

Here we also find ascending steps on the spiral staircase principle, but four-cornered as in the Temple; there, however, the structure was described as a free-standing staircase tower (see col. 30). This construction conceals a small irregularity which is possible under certain circumstances in variation B4b.

42.23ff.

It can be seen how far even the representatives of the laity were kept from the place where the cultic sacrifices were carried out.

43.?–44.3

The court is laid out with the first-fruits and their consumption on the holy days especially in mind. Yadin (I, 92f. [*I, 115*]) sees the basis for this in Dt. 14.22ff. together with 26.12f., and refers to Jubilees 22.10ff.

43.12

Here Dt. 14.24 is made more precise: it is a distance of three days' march; cf. below on 52.13f. Profane slaughter is prohibited in this zone.

43.16

In polemical fashion the author stresses that these first-fruits may not be eaten on work days. The basis for this ruling is Dt. 26.14 where we find בְאוֹנִי, often interpreted as 'in my mourning'. But in Hos. 9.1-5, where corn and wine (first-fruits?) are also mentioned, the same word also appears at v. 4. Here the frequent translation '(bread of) mourning' is unsuitable. אוֹן should be understood as 'toil/drudgery/struggle', in accordance with the LXX at Dt. 26.14 (ὀδύνη). Hos. 9.1-5 would thus be evidence that the Scroll in fact wished to adhere, by this ruling, to a very ancient practice. See Maier, *ZAW* 91, 125; Milgrom, *JQR* 71, 93f.

44.3ff

Here is given the allocation of the room units and *sukkoth* (tabernacles) sites.

The accompanying illustration shows the following: on the outside, the names of gates, and in Roman numerals the order of days at the Wood Festival; on the inside, the allocation of room units. Of the sixteen sections of portico, the two middle ones at the east (to right and left of the gate of Levi) were reserved for the sons of Aaron (priests) and after every third tribe a section is allotted to one of the three Levitical families.

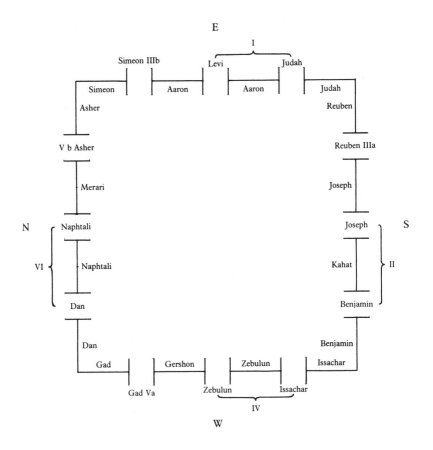

44.11

'From the corner (מקצוע) . . . ': Yadin (II, 131 [*II, 187*]) stresses that
here the measurement is taken from the 'inside corner' and not from
the 'outside corner', because, with his assumption that 1590 is an
external dimension, there is a foreshortening on the inside due to the
thickness of the wall and the 20 (or 24) cubits deep closed ancillary
buildings. The shortening did not allow a proportionate division into
fifty-four rooms in the portico section at the corner, and, for this
reason only, fifty-two room units were placed here. But this argument
is not convincing. Even in the southern section of the east side
(Judah), Yadin has to shorten the outermost room unit by the
thickness of the wall, and for Reuben's section, on the other side of
the corner, fifty-two room units (on three stories) cannot be produced,
for at least one room unit on every floor would have to be omitted.
Yadin interlocks and shortens the room units in the corners in a way
which is scarcely suitable for the plan of an ideal Temple (Fig. 1b,
p. 144). As has already been observed, the assumed corner buildings
are probably combined with kitchens (on account of the flues for the
smoke) and the fact that the number of room units at the corner is
two less (assuming that there is no scribal error!), should be seen in
this light. See further on 44.15.

44.14

The scribe first wrote מבני, 'from the sons', which would be followed
by לוי, 'of Levi'. But since the reference here is not to the members of
the tribe as a whole but to the Levites alone, the scribe erased the
letters ב and י and continued with הלויים. Cf. B. Thiering, *JBL* 100, 64.

44.15f.

The west corner (building), פנת המערב and therefore not the 'inside
corner'. Nevertheless, the same situation applies as in the south-east
corner and thus, according to Yadin's interpretation there, it would
follow that 'outside corner' is used erroneously here.

45.5-7a

Who cleanses? Those departing? The priests? Cf. Milgrom, *JQR* 71,
95.

45.7ff.

These prohibitions against entering the Temple also apply to the

Holy City, as Yadin (I, 221f. [*I, 285ff.*]) states with reference to
46.16-18 and 47.3-6. According to 45.10ff. places for those mentioned
here are to be set up outside the Holy City. The passage moves on to
the regulations for the Holy City.

45.7-10
Cf. Dt. 23.10ff.; 1QM 7.5f.

45.11-12
This ruling entails that no sexual intercourse was permitted in the
Holy City; cf. CD 12.1-2.
   Yadin (I, 223f. [*I, 288f.*]) points out that Lev. 15.18 (the first day of
uncleanness) has been amplified by analogy with the scene at Sinai in
Ex. 19.10-16. The Holy City with the Temple as the place of the
divine presence is equated with the divine mountain. On this point
see Milgrom, *JBL* 97, 516ff.

45.12-14
The blind: according to Yadin (I, 224 [*I, 289f.*]), this is an expansion
of a regulation that was originally limited to priests (Lev. 21.17; but
cf. 2 Sam. 5.8). Further, see 1QM 7.4f.; 1QSa 2.3-11 where the
presence of angels is given as the reason.

45.15-17
See Yadin I, 226f. (*I, 291ff.*): the basis is Num. 5.2f. With this cf.
Josephus, *War* 5.227; *Ant*. 3.261. Yadin postulates a combination of
prescriptions from a variety of contexts. Cf. also 46.16f. and 48.14f.
But see Milgrom, *JBL* 97, 520, for whom the basis is Lev. 15.13.

45.17
Cf. Num. 5.2-3.

46.4-5
On the protection against birds, see Yadin I, 211f. (*I, 271f.*) with
suggested restorations. But cf. also B.Z. Wacholder, *Eupolemus*, 196-
207; Eupolemus connected the installation for keeping the birds
away (cf. Josephus *War*, 5.224) with the Temple building—in fact
with the Jachin and Boaz pillars. The Scroll goes further and aims at
protecting the whole sanctuary complex.

46.5-8

רובר, 'ledge, sill, step'. Possibly only a terrace the size of the gate opening (14 × 4) placed in front of the gate is intended (Yadin, *ad loc.*). On the twelve steps of the terrace see Mishnah, *Middoth* 2.3 (Josephus, *War*, 5.193, mentions 14 steps; *Ant.* 12.427 has 'some').

46.9-12

חיל, 'embankment'. Yadin I, 145 (*I, 188ff.*) sees this as an innovation of the Scroll, but in I, 213f. (*I, 274f.*) he rightly refers to the function of the screening (cf. Ezek. 43.12). This same function was also served by a strip surrounded by a balustrade running around the Outer Court of the Herodian Temple (but set there in the 'Gentile Court'); cf. the description in Josephus (*War*, 5.193 and *Ant.* 15.417) and in the Mishnah where *Middoth* speaks of the סורג (balustrade) but *Kelim* 1.8 of the חיל. The outer Herodian enclosing structures marked the boundary of the Temple Mount, within which the 'Gentiles Court' still lay. The Scroll keeps non-Jews outside this boundary, perhaps even outside the Holy City. Cf. also Milgrom, *JQR* 71, 95f.; he renders חיל by 'moat', which is scarcely correct.

46.13-16

On the lavatories, see Yadin I, 228ff. (*I, 294ff.*). The basis for this passage is perhaps Dt. 23.13-15 (for the military camp); alternatively, both rules depend on a common older notion. Yadin refers to the traditional toilet rules, according to which the westerly direction should not be chosen for the relief of nature. To the north-west of the city this place, according to Yadin, would lie out of sight of the Temple. The relationship to the Sabbath boundaries should be noted. The lavatories lay beyond them (1QM 7 contents itself with a distance of 2000 cubits). This fits the information in Josephus (*War* 2.147) that the Essenes never relieved nature on the Sabbath. Accordingly, Yadin (I, 234f. [*I, 301ff.*]) seeks to connect the place called *bēthsô* in *War* 5.144f. with the Essene gate and to place this in the west as well. He assumes a corresponding practice for the Essenes living in Jerusalem.

Milgrom (*JQR* 71, 96ff.) remarks that ritual impurity through human excrement is implied in Ezek. 4.12-15.

46.16–47.?

The basis here is Lev. 13.46 (see Yadin I, 235f. [*I, 304f.*]). For the other cities see 48.14ff.

47.2-18

The uniformity of degrees of holiness or purity of the sacrificial
animals and their hides is strict. Rabbinic tradition treats the matter
differently: see Yadin I, 238ff. (*I, 308ff.*), citing Josephus, *Ant.*
12.146, who relates that Antiochus the Great forbade the importation
of unclean animals and skins into Jerusalem. The Scroll goes further:
the hides of clean animals might be taken to the Holy City only if
they come from sacrificed animals. In the English edition (*ad loc.* and
I, 416), Yadin states, against Ben Ḥayyim (*Leshonenu* 42, 279), that
מושקה does not mean 'drink' but 'eating vessels soaked with liquid',
and refers to 49.7-9.

47.8-9

'Bring': יביא, possibly 'come' יבואו; cf. Qimron, *IEJ* 28, 170.

Milgrom (*JQR* 71, 98) correctly points out that the prohibition
against bringing the hides of unclean animals (in the Scroll even the
hides of clean animals which had not been sacrificed) into the Holy
City provides a clue to dating. The prohibition was ratified once
again under Antiochus III (223-187 BCE) and later disappeared
completely. Here in the Scroll, as in other cases, the possibility of
pre-Maccabean subject matter should be reckoned with. The tendency,
both with Yadin and generally prevailing, towards explanation
against a Hasmonean background is in need of critical review.

47.16

Reading with Qimron (*IEJ* 28, 171) ומהר twice—once instead of יטהר.

48.?-51.18

The purity laws within this third part are given at the outset, where
they continue the same themes from the preceding part.

48.3-5

The Scroll clarifies Lev. 11.20ff. in relation to Dt. 14.20 by distinguishing between animals which go on four legs and hop or fly (which are
clean) and those that walk (which are unclean)—all locusts without
wings, for example. See the exhaustive discussion in Yadin I, 67,
247f. (*I, 79, 320f.*).

48.4

Following a corrected reading of Qimron (*IEJ* 28, 167) ההולכים (כ

written over). The deviation from the MT is thus reduced to the plural form. The reading is now accepted by Yadin, *II, 207*.

48.5

Qimron (*op. cit.*) reads מן instead of על, 'to leap up from the ground', and refers to Job 37.1.

48.5-7

According to Yadin (I, 248 [*I, 321*]), another prescription originally for priests only and deriving from Dt. 14.21, but here generalized. Cf. also Ezek. 44.31; Lev. 17.15; CD 14.3-4.

On the biblical texts, cf. also Milgrom, *JBL* 97, 520.

48.7-10

A redactional fusion (Yadin I, 63f. [*I, 74f.*]) of Lev. 21.5 (priests), Dt. 14.1-2 (all Israel) and Lev. 19.28f. (all Israel). The expression 'defile the land' provides the catchword for the addition of what follows and stands in a sort of transitional passage.

It is noteworthy that the cautionary phrase speaks of YHWH in the third person and does not, as is usually the case, have him speaking in the first person; cf. Brin, *Shnaton* 4, 212.

48.11-14

Yadin (I, 237 [*I, 395ff.*]) stresses the polemical tone and refers to the OT rulings on the cities of refuge as a stylistic model for the formulation.

48.14-17

Cf. above on the Holy City (46.16-18); but there it includes those who are unclean through emission of semen and coition. Milgrom (*JBL* 97, 513) translates: 'In every city you shall set up quarters for those afflicted with skin eruptions and scabs so that they shall not enter your cities and pollute them. The same (should be done) for gonorrheics and women in their menstrual impurity and in their parturition that they not pollute their surroundings with their impure flow'.

49.5-10

For details see Yadin I, 251f. (*I, 325ff.*). Cf. Num. 19.11-22. Num. 19.14ff. is clarified and Lev. 11.33f. is incorporated. See also 47.4-5.

49.17-19
Milgrom (*JQR* 71, 98f.) refers to 50.16-17 where it emerges that objects as well as persons had to undergo the same purification rituals.

50.4-6
Dt. 19.16 is here clarified: human bones and blood are entailed. At line 4, the restoration is supported by Qimron, *Leshonenu* 42, 145.

50.10-19
This surprisingly extensive section is constructed by analogy with the regulations for those unclean by virtue of contact with a corpse and deals with the birth of a dead child. It betrays a particular concern and polemic (Yadin I, 255f. [*I, 331f.*]). Cf. also 49.16f. In rabbinic tradition it is only the dead child that is impure and makes impure; thus it affects the midwife, but not the woman giving birth.

50.20ff.
Cf. Yadin, I, 261f. (*I, 338ff.*): here is an amplification, in which individual components are mentioned.

51.4
According to Yadin (I, 68 [*I, 79f.*]) we have here a clarification of Lev. 11.25.

51.5-10
Cf. Num. 35.34 and Lev. 11.43ff.; also 20.25; a 'conglomeration' of biblical statements (Yadin, I, 263 [*I, 342f.*]). Cf. the conclusion of 48.10f. Brin (*Shnaton* 4, 190f.) sees here a mosaic composed of Lev. 15.31 (11.43); Ex. 25.40; Num. 35.34: Lev. 11.44; 20.25; 11.43-44; 20.25 and 11.45.

The addition of בהר הזה ('on this mountain') shows to what extent the Scroll is concerned to be regarded as revelation from Sinai.

51.11ff.
Dt. 16.18ff. with Ex. 23.6 and Dt. 1.16 (see Yadin, I, 63, 68 [*I, 75, 80*]). The death penalty has been added for corruption (see Yadin, I, 292ff. [*I, 383ff.*]). Perversion of justice is understood as a form of pollution of the Land. Here the content rather than the form of the biblical text has been reproduced.

Dt. 16.19 has also undergone a transposition. On this cf. also G. Brin, *Shnaton* 4, 203ff.

52.1
Dt. 16.21? Line 2 would then be Dt. 16.22. Lines 2-3 clearly follow Lev. 26.1. Cf. Brin, *Shnaton* 4, 207f.

52.3f.
Cf. Dt 17.1.

52.6-7
Cf. Dt. 22.6 and Lev. 22.28, but with תזבח instead of תשחטו; this change, according to Milgrom (*JBL* 97, 522) is necessary because profane and sacred slaughter were subject to the same procedure.

52.7-12
Cf. Dt. 15.19-24 and Yadin, I, 243f. (*I, 314f.*).

52.11f.
Dt. 12.23f.; Lev. 17.13 and Yadin, I, 64 (*I, 75*); cf. also 53.5.

52.12-13
Dt. 25.4 (threshing); Dt. 22.10 (ox and ass).

52.13-21
Dt. 12.6ff. and Lev. 17 (see Yadin, I, 244ff. [*I, 315ff.*]). 30 *ris* are approximately 1 *parsang* = 4 miles, or 7 kilometres.

52.19-21
Dt. 12.21: see Yadin, I, 246 (*I, 318*) for traces in rabbinic tradition and also for the Karaites).

Who does the slaughtering in 52.20-21? Apparently the laymen if, according to 22.4, the Levites perform the slaughter of the sacred offerings. Cf. Milgrom, *JQR* 71, 100. The Tosephta (*Baba Kamma* 1.9) mentions only a prohibition against profane slaughter in the Temple forecourt.

53.3-4
Cf. Dt. 12.20f.

53.5f.
Dt. 12.23f. and Lev. 17.13 united into a single statement (see Yadin I, 64 [*I, 75f.*]); and cf. 52.11f.

53.7-8
Dt. 12.25 and 28.

53.9-10
Dt. 12.26 (cf. 12.11); Dt. 12.6, 11.

53.11ff.
Unification of Dt. 23.22-24 and Num. 30.3-10.

54.5-7
Dt. 13.1.

54.6
'You' may be singular or plural: אותמה or אותכה is added above the line, partially illegible (Qimron, *IEJ* 28, 167).

54.8-18
Dt. 13.2-6.

54.19–55.1
Dt. 13.7-12.

55.2-14
Dt. 13.13-19. Note particularly the insertion of 'all'. On the use of Dt. 13.13ff. see Brin, *Shnaton* 4, 210-212. It is noteworthy that there is no change to the first person here (cf. 63.3-8); in Dt. 13.18 the oath form is avoided (because of anthropomorphism?). Milgrom (*JQR* 71, 100) sees in this no change of content.

55.15-21
Dt. 17.2-5.

56.?-11
Dt. 17.8-13.

56.3ff.
What is intended by 'Torah'? Z. Falk (*Sinai* 83, 30ff., 36f.) thinks that

it might be the 'oral Torah' and refers to Mishnah, *Sanhedrin* 2. Brin (*Shnaton* 4, 184f.), however, correctly stresses that the concern here is above all with the giving of the Torah through priestly authority.

56.8f.

Note the transposition in Dt. 17.12. According to Milgrom (*JBL* 97, 522), the purpose is to reinforce the preceding admonition.

56.10

The MT at Dt. 17.12 has ומת, the Scroll יומת, making it clear that execution is intended; cf. Qimron, *IEJ* 28, 170; Brin, *Shnaton* 4, 185.

56.12–60.?

Royal authority: see Yadin, I, 264ff. (*I, 344ff.*). The Scroll contains characteristic additions which are more wide-ranging than the text of Dt. 17.14-20. In particular they deal with the guard, the royal council, the queen, the division of spoil, and the various ways of obtaining priestly oracles. Yadin sees in this a reflection of conditions under the Hasmoneans. But if this were the case one would certainly expect a clear polemic against the union of the roles of High Priest and Prince (King) in one person.

Yadin and M. Weinfeld (*Shnaton* 3, 214ff.) are inclined to see in this section a special 'Tractate for the King', the 'Law' which he had to read aloud at Sukkoth. On the other hand, Z. Falk (*Sinai* 83, 30f.) sees in this only a statement of the power entrusted in the king whereby, on the basis of the text of the Torah, it is the oral tradition in particular that comes into play. D. Mendels (*Shnaton* 3, 245ff.; *Aegyptus* 59, 127ff.) compares the details that concern the king with the contents of the *Letter of Aristeas* and comes to the conclusion that older Jewish ideas about the king have been adopted in the *Letter of Aristeas* with a Hellenizing interpretation in which Ptolemaic conditions had a profound influence. Now Weinfeld (*RB* 87, 394ff.) has also claimed that there are Ptolemaic parallels in the Scroll (see on 57.5-11). In my opinion (as already expressed at 47.7ff.) this raises the question of dating. The explanation of this view of royal authority (whether in a 'Tractate of the King' or not) as a reaction to Hasmonean kingship is not convincing. In all cases we could be dealing with material that was already generally available in the third century. The close relations of the Oniads and Tobiads to the Ptolemaic court could also have played a role when it came to actualizing the royal power described in Deuteronomy, perhaps in connection with the hopes for independence during the Diadoche feuds and the persistent disputes between the Seleucids and the Ptolemies. On all this see M. Delcor, *Henoch* 3, 47ff. His translation of 56.15f., however, is scarcely tenable: 'et il ne fera pas revenir le peuple d'Egypte en vue de la guerre . . . ' (49-50). See also Yadin, *I, 41*).

56.16-18
The obscure reference to 'leading back to Egypt' in Dt. 17.16 is clarified with the addition 'to battle' (Yadin, I, 66 [*I, 80*]: 'halachic explanation'). Z. Falk (*Sinai* 83, 31f.) suggests that the Scroll rejects any return to Egypt, whether for war or commerce, and that this is evidently to be seen against the background of discussion about the legitimacy of settling in Egypt that had persisted since the time of Jeremiah (Jer. 42.7). But here too the situation under Ptolemaic rule and the period of the wars between the Seleucids and the Ptolemies should be considered.

56.18f.
Again the Scroll clarifies the biblical text: the many women are the subject of the subordinate clause; they turn the king's heart away from God (cf. Yadin I, 66 [*I, 78f.*]).

56.20f.
'This Torah', not, as in Dt. 17.18, preceded by משנה; cf. also 57.1. Obviously the text of the Torah in the Temple Scroll is intended (see Yadin, I, 70f., 264f. [*I, 83, 344ff.*]), and in fact probably only the Torah of the king's authority, not the whole Pentateuch.

The Scroll has בשבתו for MT כשבתו and plural כתבו ('they'). This makes it clear that the king does not do the writing himself (as Mishnah, *Sanhedrin* 2.4; *Targum Onkelos* to Dt. 17.18; *Targum Neofiti, ad loc.*; however, the plural is also found in *Targum Pseudo-Jonathan*).

56.21
'The Levites' has been omitted, probably to avoid the misunderstanding that they might be included.

57.1-11a
The military system. According to Falk (*Sinai* 83, 33) this is a 'midrash-like' use of biblical passages for a new purpose. Weinfeld's reference (*RB* 87, 394ff.) to the description of Ptolemaic conditions by Diodorus Siculus (= Hecataeus of Abdera) is important.

57.1-3
Cf. Yadin, I, 266 (*I, 346f.*). The priests clearly called this muster (in Num 1.3 it is Moses and Aaron). In line 3 the text was corrected; the scribe first wrote the plural, then the suffix was rubbed out so that the king became the subject. Scribal error (so Yadin), or correction of content?

57.2
According to Milgrom (*JQR* 71, 100), ביום, 'on the day', does not have to indicate the day of coronation; it could mean 'thereafter'.

57.3
The limits of 20–60 years follows Lev. 27.3. For further particulars about the stages of life see Yadin, I, 266 (*I, 347*).

57.3-4
According to Milgrom (*JBL* 97, 522f.) this depends on Dt. 20.9, with the prescription taken from the civil to the military sphere, since the Hasmoneans did, after all, have a standing army and not a civilian militia.

57.5-11
The number of 12,000 men for the standing army depends on Num. 31.4f. But here the army is pointedly described as the king's guard who were to prevent his falling into enemy hands. If, as Yadin assumes, this section reflects Hasmonaean conditions, then the possibility of an immediate effect of the shock caused by the capture and subsequent execution of Jonathan Maccabaeus should be considered. But this is uncertain; everything that is laid down about the king's authority can be interpreted quite happily without reference to a Hasmonaean background. Yadin (I, 267f. [*I, 348f.*]) feels that the system of selecting only Israelites was directed not least against the practice of hiring mercenaries that John Hyrcanus had established (Josephus, *Ant.* 13.249, 304, 374). Furthermore, in *Ant.* 13.311f., Essene prophecy is said to play a role in this connection; the matter is

therefore open to considerable discussion. Taken together, all this would make John Hyrcanus a strong candidate for the 'Wicked Priest'. However, with regard to the possibility of capture, Yadin's reference (I, 267 [*I, 348f.*]) to Alexander Jannaeus in *Ant.* 13.375 as a parallel seems to me to present a chronological difficulty.

Weinfeld (*RB* 87, 394ff.) has shown several parallels with the description of the Ptolemaic royal guard in Diodorus Siculus, and sees in the Scroll a corroboration of Diodorus's information. Both sources 'reflect royal ideologies prevalent in Judah and Egypt in the Hellenistic period'. The number 12,000 would perhaps depend on Num. 31.3f. (so Yadin) with 1 Kings 10.26 and 2 Kings 11.8ff.

The linguistic criterion for dating that Brin has frequently invoked (*Shnaton* 4, 198f.) is problematic. At issue is the significanc of 'non-biblical' and hence even 'late' diction in the Scroll. But what date does such 'late' diction actually imply? Indeed, many ancient Hebrew inscriptions would be deemed 'late' on this criterion, because they contain non-biblical words, etc. Here, too, Falk tries to harmonize with rabbinic tradition (*Sinai* 83, 33), even though he does stress how lines 9-10 differ from Mishnah *Sanhedrin* 2.4.

57.11-15

The royal council (see Yadin, I, 269f. [*I, 349ff.*]) consists of twelve priests, twelve Levites and twelve laymen; thus there were thirty-six members. Here Dt. 17.20 ('he shall not raise himself above his brothers') has been used to create an institution: the king is bound by the decisions of the Royal Council. With regard to the individual subjects of the realm, see the king's legal obligations below, lines 19-21.

Falk (*Sinai* 83, 34) sees in the total of thirty-six a majority in the Sanhedrin, which had a full complement of seventy-one. The uniform representation of laymen, Levites and priests is surprising; Milgrom (*JBL* 97, 502) considers 2 Chron. 19.5-11 as a possible model. In addition, see Baumgarten, *JBL* 95 (1976), 59-78.

57.15-19

The queen (see Yadin I, 270ff. [*I, 353ff.*]) cannot be a non-Jew; this precludes the possibility of any political marriage. Yadin detects here a polemic against Hasmonaean practice (a chronologically difficult proposal). More characteristic, because it also contradicts rabbinic tradition (Tosephta, *Sanhedrin* 4.2), is the stipulation that the queen

should come from the king's family. According to Yadin, Gen. 24.37f.
and Num. 36.6-8 would have served as the biblical basis for this law.
More plausibly, he also refers to the well-known attempt to draw a
parallel with the High Priest (cf. Lev. 21.13-15, particularly according
to the LXX). This is also appropriate to the mention of the two
'anointed ones' common elsewhere in the Dead Sea Scrolls. Also
specifically Qumranic is the prohibition against having two or more
wives. This ruling would also seem, possibly, to exclude divorce; cf.,
in general, CD 4.19–5.5. Whether this also held true in the event of
childlessness must remain an open question. But remarriage after the
death of a wife is clearly provided for, and hence was presumably
permissible to everyone. On the other hand, it should be borne in
mind that in lines 17f. the formulation follows Lev. 18.18 (see Yadin,
ad loc.), i.e. an incest law, so that the prohibition against the king's
taking a second wife (who would have to be from his own family) in
addition to the first should be understood not so much in terms of
monogamy as of an extended sexual taboo. Falk (*Sinai* 83, 35f.) refers
to the High Priest's obligation to monogamy according to rabbinic
tradition (Bab. Talmud, *Yoma* 13a).

This section also separates 57.11-15a from 19-21 in a striking
fashion.

57.20f.
Here the king is subject to generally accepted law (in contrast to the
Hellenistic conception). The stress on property agrees with the
common denouncement at Qumran of unjust wealth (cf. 1QpHab
8.10 and 9.4 where Maccabean practices are apparently intended).

58.10
Cf. the difference in the qualification in lines 16f.

58.11
'Conquer', נצחו: its earliest attestation otherwise is in Talmudic
Hebrew, but Yadin, *ad loc*, refers to 1QM 4.13 where the noun נצח
occurs, apparently with the meaning 'victory'.

58.11-15
The division of spoil; cf. Yadin, I, 64, 275ff. (*I, 76, 358ff.*). The Scroll
resolves the contradiction between Num. 31.27f. and 1 Sam. 30.24f.
by giving a tenth to the king immediately, from the remainder a

thousandth to the priests and a hundredth to the Levites, and from
what is then left those who took part in the war and those who
formed the home guard each receive their allotted share. The king's
tenth, mentioned in 1 Sam. 8.15-17, is made to apply to the soldiers
as well. Yadin (I, 275f. [*I, 360*]) refers to Gen. 14.20 for an example of
booty-tithe. See also the references given below at 60.4f., 7f. Z. Falk
(*Sinai* 83, 38) refers to Mishnah, *Sanhedrin* 2.4. Milgrom (*JBL* 97,
520f.) corrects the calculations in Yadin: the difference between the
shares of the fighting units and those of the units on the home front is
only nine-thousandths, but nevertheless the Scroll, in accordance
with 1 Sam 30.24f., insists on exact division.

58.15ff.
Offensive action is strictly under the control of the High Priest's
oracular direction (11.18-21). Cf. Num. 27.17-21; 1QM 8.8f. This
concern is indirectly emphasized by the concluding sequence of
blessings and curses which follows immediately. For the literary
form and stylistic correspondences see particularly Dt. 28. This
whole section is a mosaic of biblical motifs; see the detailed examples
in Yadin, *ad loc.*

58.17
Qimron (*IEJ* 28, 169) reads עריות instead of ערוות.

59.2-15
According to Brin (*Shnaton* 4, 191f.) this is a composite section of
admonitions from the following biblical texts together with curses
and blessings, used freely: (2) Dt. 28.36-7, 64; (3-4) Dt. 4.28, 36, 48;
(4-5) Lev. 26.31f.; (6) Zech. 7.13; Jer. 11.11; (7) Dt. 31.18; Jer. 21.12;
(7/8) Ezek. 34.4, 8; 2 Kings 21.14; (8) Dt. 28.29; Jer. 44.3; (8/9)
Lev. 26.15, 43; (9/10) Hos. 5.15: 6.1; 3.5; (10) Dt. 30.14; 17.19;
(11/12) Dt. 31.21; Jer. 25.9; (12) Zech. 10.8; Dt. 28.63; (13) Lev. 26.12;
Jer. 31.31; Ezek. 37.27.

59.9
Milgrom (*JQR* 71, 102) translates 'until they are thoroughly punished'
(based on Hos. 5.15), referring to the climax of Israel's suffering.

59.13
לעם: see on 29.7; Brin (*Shnaton* 4, 220f.) reads לעולם, referring to Jer.
31.32f.

60.?-15

The claims of the cult officials (see Yadin, I, 124, 127f. [*I, 159f., 163ff.*]) are laid down here in accordance with Dt. 18.1-8, but with additions from Lev. 27, Num. 18 and 31. The text first describes what the priests receive and then the Levites' share but with lines 9-11 as an addendum.

60.2

Qimron (*Leshonenu* 42, 145) and Milgrom (*JQR* 71, 102f.) offer the improved reading and restoration בכ[ורותי]חמה. Because it concerns the priests' privileges, Milgrom (*op cit.*) sees this passage as a contradiction to 52.7-12 where, following Dt. 15.19-23, the owners are allowed to eat the sacrificed first-born. Did the Scroll interpret תאכלנו in Dt. 15.20 as referring to the priests? But perhaps this is not the problem at all, if in 60.2 only the priestly portion is meant, rather than the whole of it.

60.3-5

Hillulim, the contribution which was due every fourth year according to Lev. 19.24; cf. Jubilees 7.36 (differently in rabbinic tradition). The linguistic use of מכס, 'contributed portion' in the sense of a regular contribution, should be noted here and in lines 7-9. Yadin, I, 129 (*I, 167*) notes that the biblical term is אהו (cf. Num. 31.47). Compare and contrast 58.12-14. In the Bible מכס is already found in the text of Num. 31.28 as meaning a portion of the spoils of war; this usage has been taken up here in line 5 after the addition of 'and from everything that they have placed under a ban' (cf. Lev. 27.28; Num. 18.14; Ezek. 4.29). Yadin (I, 128 [*I, 166ff.*]) suspects a polemic, for in the rabbinic tradition there are other evaluations.

60.6-7

See 20.15ff. and Rockefeller Museum fragment 43.975, line c. The basis is Num. 18.21ff. Yadin, I, 125f. (*I, 160ff.*) feels that the expansion comes directly from Neh. 13.5; 10.12 (but perhaps the views are merely similar?) combined with a reminiscence of Lev. 27.30. It thus deals with what the Rabbis called the 'first tithe' and the biblical texts quoted were interpreted accordingly. This offering should be distinguished from the 'second tithe'. See Dt. 14.22-26; 26.12f., and col. 43. The 'levitical tithe' became obsolete in the course of the Second Temple period, or more precisely, it was usurped by the priests. The Scroll represents the older ruling. Cf. Milgrom, *JBL* 97, 502, 519f.

60.7
On the shoulder as the Levites' portion see above on 20.15ff. See also the discussion devoted to this in Milgrom, *JBL* 97, 504ff.

60.9-10
The passage concerning the doves is marked by a clumsy insertion. Yadin, I, 129f. (*I, 167f.*) conjectures a polemic against a precise demand for a honey tithe. The honey is that of wild bees and hence, like the wild doves, is regarded as hunted game. On the disagreement with rabbinic tradition see Yadin, *loc. cit.*

60.10-11
Dt. 18.5 rearranged—but cf. the LXX. Yadin (I, 130 [*I, 168*]) feels that priests and Levites together are intended, but cf. 63.3f. Milgrom (*JBL* 97, 523) also assumes that 'to serve and bless my name' applies to the priests as well as the Levites. But this is not at all convincing, for the passage can apply most plausibly to the priests who were the last to be given particular prominence. Certainly Milgrom interprets לשרת in connection with Levites in 60.14 (*JBL* 97, 503) as 'to assist' (cf. also *JQR* 71, 103f.), especially since there Dt. 18.7 has been correspondingly altered. Therefore, according to Milgrom, there could be no question of the Levites' officiating in altar service.

60.15
'Apart from the proceeds inherited from the fathers' (ממכר על לבד האבות). In Dt. 18.5 the MT reads ממכריו. The precise meaning of this technical term is disputed. It is scarcely to be identified with מכר (e.g. Neh. 13.16) or to be connected with ממכר (cf. Lev. 25.14). It is more likely to be an expression for a form of revenue peculiar to the priests or Levites. See on this Maier, *Judaica* 26, 89-105 (89ff.); M. Cohn, *VT* 31, 472-82.

60.16-20
Cf. Dt. 18.9-13.

60.18
At the end of the line read שואל אוב instead of באוב.

60.21a

This is the end of Dt. 18.14, but not rewritten in the first person!

60.21–61.?

Cf. Dt. 18.14-19. A suggested reconstruction is given in Yadin, *ad loc.*).

61.?-5

Cf. Dt. 18.20-22. The passive והומת in line 2 makes it clear that the death penalty is meant. Note that in what follows Dt. 19.1-14 is skipped over, because the false witness is discussed immediately after the false prophet by linking catchwords. The division of sentences is difficult; see Brin, *Shnaton* 4, 183f. Possibly the interrogative is being continued.

61.2

At the end this should be read נרע את הדבר, following the MT.

61.4

This should also be read, following the MT, הוא הדבר; and לוא אשר דברתי instead of דברתיו). See Qimron, *IEJ* 28, 168; Milgrom, *JBL* 97, 523.

61.6-12

Dt. 19.15-21. The Levites have been explicitly added to Dt. 19.17. In line 8, לויים refers to the cult functionaries, not the members of the tribe of Levi in general.

61.12–63.?

Martial law; cf. Dt. 20.1-18 (note the LXX!).

61.14

Reading כקרובבכמה instead of כקרבכה with Qimron, *IEJ* 28, 168.

62.6

'Then you shall call upon it . . . ', reading וקראתה אליה instead of עליה after Qimron (*ibid.*).

63.?-9

Expiation rite for murder by person or persons unknown; Dt. 21.1-9 (cf. LXX!).

63.5
The hands were therefore washed over the head of the heifer (cf. LXX and see Yadin, *ad loc.*).

63.10–64.?
A female slave captured in war as wife; cf. Dt. 21.10-14, substantially amplified here. In Dt. 21.12-13a, the man is the subject here, as also in the LXX.

63.13-15 An addition to the biblical text; see Yadin, I, 68, 279f. (*I, 80f., 364ff.*). The seven year purity prohibition brings to mind the seven year penalty of CD 12.5f. It is not clear (see Yadin, I, 281 [*I, 368*]), whether the prohibition against eating sacrificial flesh is to be calculated additionally to the original 7 years. On exclusion from a degree of purity cf. 1QS 5.13ff.; 6.16ff.; etc.

63.14-15
On the language cf. Brin, *Leshonenu* 43, 24-26; *Shnaton* 4, 193f., for whom the stylistic basis is Lev. 15.28; 22.4, 6f., but the content is 'sectarian'. On this point see also Milgrom, *JQR* 71, 104f. Whereas Yadin (*ad loc.*) discusses the possibility of two periods of seven years, Milgrom considers a possible analogy with the 7/8 day limit for purification. According to the Scroll, the state of purity is only restored on the eighth day after a sacrifice has been made. Similarly, the prohibition against eating ritually pure food would last until the seventh year, that against the flesh of a sacrifice until the eighth.

64.?-6
Dt. 21.18-21.

64.2
Slight improvements in the reading are given by Qimron, *IEJ* 28, 168; *Leshonenu* 42, 145.

64.5
'And rebellious'—ומורר instead of ומורה.

64.6-9
Crucifixion as the penalty for treason. Whether 'to hang on the wood' is precisely the same as 'to crucify' is queried by Baumgarten, *Studies*

in Qumran Law, 172-82, but Yadin (*ad loc.* and I, 285ff. [*I, 373ff.*]) is doubtless correct when he considers this distinction to be relatively unimportant. What is significant is that this is the most dishonourable form of death penalty, which is specifically imposed for a political crime, treason against the people. For echoes in rabbinic tradition, which replaced this death penalty with strangulation, see Heinemann, *'Aggadot*, 148ff. For the relationship with the NT cf. J.M. Ford, *ET* 87, 275-78. Yadin (I, 285ff. [*I, 373ff.*]) takes Lev. 19.16 as a formal model and considers events in the early second century BCE as the motivation. Hanging is clearly the cause of death, as a comparison of the word order with that of Dt. 21.22 shows (in rabbinic interpretation the corpse of a man executed by stoning was also hanged on a post).

Yadin (I, 289f. [*I, 378ff.*]) believes it possible to interpret the passage in 4QpNahum dealing with the 'Lion of Anger' differently from the usual manner. This figure hung his domestic political opponents 'alive on wood', and the allusion is obviously to Alexander Jannaeus's mass execution of Pharisees. Whereas interpreters have usually understood this as a criticism of Jannaeus, Yadin feels that the lacuna in the text should be restored so that in this context the passage states that the Angry Lion had them hanged on the wood, 'as it is the law in Israel'—i.e. as the penalty for treason, since they had sought help from a Seleucid ruler against their own king. Yadin suggests that since only the type of death penalty is at issue in 4QpNahum, no reproach is intended; this inference, he claims, the Scroll now supports. But Yadin's explanation does not, of course, determine whether or not the author of 4QpNahum nevertheless wished to condemn the spectacle of mass execution —by whatever means—staged by Alexander Jannaeus.

Recent discussion sometimes starts from the fact that we are dealing with an interpretation of the biblical text; cf. M.J. Bernstein, *Gesher* 7, 145-66. Brin (*Shnaton* 4, 201f.) correctly emphasizes that two distinct offences are named: treason, and fleeing to foreigners after committing a capital offence and thus cursing one's own people. In line 10 תליתמה גם אותו על העץ ('you should hang also him on the wood') is allegedly a late linguistic formulation (as compared, for instance, to Ex. 21.29). But what does 'late' actually mean? L. Rosso, *RQ* 9, 231-36, on the contrary, sees in the Scroll a reading of the biblical text that was later suppressed.

In the Aramaic inscription from the floor mosaic at En-Gedi (6th century BCE) a similar offence is mentioned, and is commended to divine punishment by a curse. For the text see Naveh, *On Mosaic and Stone*, 106f.; Y. Israeli in E. Carmon and R. Grafman, *Inscriptions Reveal*, 188-91, with English translation in the English part, p. 85: '... Whosoever shall sow (lit. give) discord between a man and his colleague, or denounce his colleague to the Gentiles, or steal belongings of his colleague, or whosoever shall reveal the secret of the town to the Gentiles—may He whose eyes range over the entire earth and sees the hidden, He shall set his face against that person and his seed, and shall uproot (עקר) him from under the heavens. And the entire people say: Amen, amen. Selah!'

Crimes of this nature doubtless gave rise to the practical application formulated in the Scroll many centuries before in the light of Dt. 21.22f. No offence is named there, but only the execution and the time of the burial is fixed. Brin (*Shnaton* 4, 201) gives 1 Sam. 27.11 as a possible model for the applied ruling; but there the killing is a precaution, to prevent a (faithful!) report. One scarcely needs to seek out biblical models for such legal formulation. Rather it developed out of practical experience and could even have played a role in the disputes between the pro-Ptolemaic and pro-Seleucid parties in the Seleucid–Maccabaean period.

64.9-11

It is not clear—and probably not relevant—whether flight before or after trial is intended. What is significant here is that again it is treason which has been committed, leading to the application of the most dishonourable form of execution.

64.11-13

Cf. Dt. 21.22-23 with the clarification that a person hanged on the wood is one cursed by God and men. Cf. the LXX 'cursed of God' (Gal. 3.13), and see Yadin, I, 289f. (*I, 379*).

64.13–65.?

The lost cattle of a fellow Israelite: cf. Dt. 22.1-3.

65.?-5

Taking from a bird's nest (Dt. 22.6-7) is at first sight a surprising topic, since the author has elsewhere departed from the order of Deuteronomy when he wanted to bring together material of similar content. Obviously he did not understand the text as being primarily

one designed to maintain the
aelites. An infringement against
inst a fellow Israelite, and fit the

ι reading 'his' instead of 'your' roof.

υ..

Reading עלות ..... . In line 7 בעלה instead of בא אליה in Dt.
2.13 is a feature of late language according to Brin, *Leshonenu* 43, 24.

65.10

בתול, singular instead of plural—perhaps a scribal error (Yadin, *ad loc.*) since in line 13f. the plural is used.

65.15

This provides the reason which justifies the law in this context.

66.?-11

Cf. Dt. 22.23-9.

66.4-5

The contents of Dt. 22.25 are substantially clarified. Instead of בשדה ('in the open countryside'/'in an un-built-up area') the Scroll paraphrases so as to describe a situation that is precisely the *opposite* of an incident within a built-up area! The same judicial clarification was produced by Josephus (*Ant.* 4.252) with different wording.

As is frequently the case, the *hoph'al* והומת has been substituted for MT ומת in line 25, to make it clear that the offender is to be executed.

66.7ff.

The spaces between the lines vary somewhat in width at this point.

66.8-11

This is a stipulation skilfully combining Ex. 22.15f. and Dt. 22.28. The seduced woman and the violated woman are thus subject to the same law (see Yadin, I, 65 [*I, 76f.*). Yadin, I, 281ff. (*I, 368ff.*) offers a synopsis of the two biblical passages in comparison with the formulation here.

Attention should be paid to the expression 'permitted to him by law' (רויה לו מן החוק), for which Yadin refers to Mishnah, *Ketuboth* 3.5, etc. Cf. also 2Q3 (DJD III, 54).

66.11-17

The incest laws, which break off in line 17, are compiled from various biblical sources and are occasioned by Dt. 23.1, where only the father's wife is mentioned, thus giving the impression of being incomplete. Here the biblical law is expanded to include the brother's wife (cf. Lev. 20.21), the sister (cf. Lev. 20.17; Dt. 27.22), the aunt (cf. Lev. 18.12f.; 20.19), and the niece (cf. CD 5.7). See also Yadin, I, 284f. (*I, 371ff.*).

The text, which is not carried over to column 67, would have continued with Dt. 23.1ff.

BIBLIOGRAPHY

General Works on Qumran

Bibliographies
Burchardt, C. *Bibliographie zu den Handschriften vom Toten Meer*, 2 vols, Berlin, 1957/1965
Jongeling, B. *A Classified Bibliography of the Finds in the Desert of Judah 1958-1969*, Leiden, 1971
Fitzmyer, J.A. *The Dead Sea Scrolls. Major publications and tools for study*, Missoula, 1977[2]

Introductions
Vermes, G. *The Dead Sea Scrolls*, London, 1977
Soggin, J.A. *I Manoscritti del Mar Morto*, Rome, 1978

Text editions
Discoveries in the Judean Desert I, III-VII, Oxford 1955-1982.
Burrows, M. *The Dead Sea Scrolls of the St. Mark's Monastery*, New Haven, 1950 (1QIs[a]; 1QpHab)
—*Plates and Transcription of the Manual of Discipline*, New Haven, 1951 (1QS)
Sukenik, E.L. *The Dead Sea Scrolls of the Hebrew University*, Jerusalem, 1955 (1QIs[b]; 1QM; 1QH)
Avigad, N. & Yadin, Y. *A Genesis Apocryphon*, Jerusalem, 1956 (1QGenAp)
van der Ploeg, J.P.M., van der Woude, A.S. & Jongeling, B. *Le Targum de Job*, Leiden, 1971 (11QTgJob)
Yadin, Y. מגילת־המקרש, 3 vols., Jerusalem, 1978; ET *The Temple Scroll*, Jerusalem, 1984
Zeitlin, S. *The Zadokite Fragments*, Philadelphia, 1952 (CD)
Rabin, C. *The Zadokite Documents*, Oxford, 1958 (CD)
Adam, A. *Antike Berichte über die Essener*, Berlin 1972[2]

Selected important monographs
Baumgarten, J.M. *Studies in Qumran Law*, Leiden, 1977
Becker, J. *Das Heil Gottes*, Göttingen, 1964
Black, M. (ed.) *The Scrolls and Christianity*, London, 1969
Cross, F.M. & Talmon, S. *Qumran and the History of the Biblical Text*, Cambridge, Mass., 1975
Davies, P.R. *The Damascus Covenant*, Sheffield, 1983
Delcor, M. (ed.) *Qumran*, Louvain, 1978
Driver, G.R. *The Judaean Scrolls*, Oxford, 1965
Forkman, G. *The Limits of Religious Community*, Lund, 1972
Gabrion, H. 'L'interprétation de l'écriture dans la littérature de Qumran',

Aufsteig und Niedergang des römischen Weltreiches II/19.1, Berlin, 1979, 779-848

Garnet, P. *Salvation and Atonement in the Qumran Scrolls*, Tübingen, 1977

Gioia, F. *La comunità di Qumran*, Rome, 1979

Horgan, M.P. *Pesharim: Qumran Interpretations of Biblical Books*, Washington, 1979

Jeremias, G. *Der Lehrer der Gerechtigkeit*, Göttingen, 1963

Klinzing, G. *Die Umdeutung des Kultus in der Qumrangemeinde und im Neuen Testament*, Göttingen, 1971

Kuhn, H.-W. *Enderwartung und gegenwärtiges Heil*, Göttingen, 1966

Laperrousaz, E.-M. *Qoumrân*, Paris, 1976

—*L'Attente du Messie*, Paris 1982

Le Moyne, J. *Les Sadducéens*, Paris, 1972

Lichtenberger, H. *Studien zum Menschenbild in Texten der Qumrangemeinde*, Tübingen, 1980

Merrill, E.H. *Qumran and Predestination*, Leiden, 1975

Moraldi, L. *Il maestro di giustizia*, Fassano, 1972

Muszyński, H. *Fundament, Bild und Metapher in den Handschriften aus Qumran*, Rome, 1975

Ringgren, H. *The Faith of Qumran*, Philadelphia, 1963

Sanders, E.P. *Paul and Palestinian Judaism*, London, 1973

Schiffman, L.H., *The Halakhah at Qumran*, Leiden, 1975

Schwarz, E. *Identität durch Abgrenzung*, Berne/Frankfurt, 1981

Thyen, H. *Studien zur Sündenvergebung im Neuen Testament*, Göttingen, 1970

The Temple Scroll

Text

Yadin, Y. מגילת־המקדש, 3 vols., Jerusalem, 1978 (ET *The Temple Scroll*, Jerusalem, 1984)

Caquot, A. 'Le Rouleau du Temple de Qoumrân', *Études Théologiques et Religieuses* 53 (1978), 443-500 (French translation)

Studies

Baumgarten, J.M. *Studies in Qumran Law*, Leiden, 1977

—'The Duodecimal Courts of Qumran, Revelation and the Sanhedrin', *JBL* 95 (1976), 59-78

—'Hanging and Treason in Qumran and Roman Law', *Eretz Israel* 16 (1982), 7-16

Bernstein, M.J. 'Midrash Halakhah at Qumran?', *Gesher* 7 (1979), 145-66

Blidstein, G. '4Q Florilegium and Rabbinic Sources on Bastard and Proselyte', *RQ* 8 (1974), 431-35

Brin, G. 'הערות לשוניות למגילת־המקדש', *Leshonenu* 43 (1979), 20-28

—'The Bible as Reflected in the Temple Scroll', *Shnaton* 4 (1979-80), 182-225

Busink, T.A. *Der Tempel von Jerusalem* II, Leiden, 1980, 1424-26

Carmon, E. and Grafman, R. *Inscriptions Reveal*, Jerusalem, 1973

Cohn, M. '*mᵉkērōtēhem* (Genèse xlix 5)', *VT* 31 (1981), 472-82

Delcor, M. 'Le statut du roi d'après le Rouleau du Temple', *Henoch* 3 (1981), 47-68

Dimant, D. 'Jerusalem and the Temple according to the Animal Apocalypse (1 Enoch 85-90) in the Light of the Ideology of the Dead Sea Sect', *Shnaton* 5-6 (1982), 177-93

Falk, Z. 'מגילת־המקרש והמשנה הרישונה', *Sinai* 83 (1977-78), 30-41

—'The Temple Scroll and the Codification of Jewish Law', *Jewish Law Annual* 2 (1979), 33-44

Flusser, D. Review of Y. Yadin, *Megillat ham-miqdash*, *Numen* 26 (1979), 271-74

Ford, J.M. '"Crucify him" and the Temple Scroll' *ET* 87 (1976), 275-78

Heinemann, J. אגרות ותולדותיהן, Jerusalem, 1974

Jongeling, B. 'De "Tempelrol"', *Phoenix* 25 (1979), 84-99

Kaufman, S. A., 'The Temple Scroll and Higher Criticism', *HUCA* 53 (1982), 29-43

Kimron: see Qimron

Küchler, M. *Frühjüdische Weisheitstraditionen*, Freiburg/Göttingen, 1979

Laperrousaz, E.-M. 'Note à propos de la datation du Rouleau du Temple et généralement des manuscrits de la Mer Morte', *RQ* 10 (1980-81), 447-52

Levine, B.A., 'The Temple Scroll—Aspects of its Historical Provenance and Literary Character', *BASOR* 232 (1979), 5-23

Maier, J. 'Die sog. Tempelrolle von Qumran', *ZAW* 78 (1966), 152-54

— 'Bemerkungen zur Fachsprache und Religionspolitik im Königreich Judah', *Judaica* 26 (1970), 89-105

—'Ergänzend zu Jes 62,9', *ZAW* 91 (1979), 125

—'Aspekte der Kultfrömmigkeit im Lichte der Tempelrolle von Qumran', in H.H. Henrix, *Jüdische Liturgie*, Freiburg, 1979, 33-46

—'Die Hofanlagen im Tempelentwurf des Ezechiel im Licht der 'Tempelrolle' von Qumran', in *Prophecy. Essays presented to Georg Fohrer* (BZAW, 150), Berlin, 1980, 55-67

Mendels, D. '"On Kingship" in the "Temple Scroll" and the Ideological Vorlage of the Seven Banquets in the "Letter of Aristeas to Philocrates"', *Aegyptus* 59 (1979), 127-36

Milgrom, J. 'The Temple Scroll', *BA* 41 (1978), 105-20

—'הערות על מגילת־המקרש', *Beth Miqra* 23 (1977-78), 494-507

—'Studies in the Temple Scroll', *JBL* 97 (1978), 501-23

—'הערות למגילת־המקרש', *Beth Miqra* 24 (1978-79), 205-11

—'Further Studies in the Temple Scroll,' *JQR* 71 (1980-81), 1-17, 89-106

Mink, H.A. 'Praesentation af et nyt Qumranskrift: Tempelrullen', *Dansk Teologisk Tidsskrift* 42 (1979), 81-112

Mishor, M. 'On the Version of the Temple Scroll', *Tarbiz* 48 (1978-9), 173

Mueller, J.R., 'The "Temple Scroll" and the Gospel Divorce Texts', *RQ* 10 (1980-81), 247-56

Naveh, J. *On Mosaic and Stone*, Jerusalem, 1978

Polzin, R. *Late Biblical Hebrew*, New Haven, 1976

Qimron, E. 'New Readings in the Temple Scroll', *IEJ* 28 (1978), 161-72

—'לנסחה של מגילת־המקדש', *Leshonenu* 42 (1978), 136-45

—'לשונה של מגילת־המקדש', *Leshonenu* 42 (1978), 83-98

—'The Vocabulary of the Temple Scroll,' *Shnaton* 4 (1979-80), 239-62

—'Three Notes on the Text of the Temple Scroll', *Tarbiz* 51 (1981-82), 135-137

—'The Word KWNNH', *Tarbiz* 52 (1982-83), 133

Rokeah, D. 'Essene Notes', *Shnaton* 4 (1979-80), 263-68

—'Addendum to "Essene Notes"', *Shnaton* 5-6 (1982), 231

Rosso, L. 'Deuteronomio 21,22; contributo del Rotolo del Tempio alla valutazione di una variante medievale dei Settanta', *RQ* 9 (1977), 231-236

Sacchi, P. 'Scoperto di un nuovo rotolo in Palestina (Rotolo di tempio)', *Rivista di Storia e Letteratura Religiosa* 3 (1967), 579-80

Schiffman, L.H. 'The Temple Scroll in Literary and Philological Perspective', in W.S. Green (ed.), *Approaches to Ancient Judaism II*, Chico, 1980, 143-58

Stegemann, H. 'Die Bedeutung der Qumranfunde für die Erforschung der Apokalyptik', in D. Hellholm (ed.), *Apocalypticism*, Tübingen, 1983, 495-530

Thiering, B. '*Mebaqqer* and *Episkopos* in the Light of the Temple Scroll', *JBL* 100 (1981), 59-74

Tov, E. 'The "Temple Scroll" and Old Testament Textual Criticism', *Eretz Israel* 16 (1982), 100-11

Wacholder, B.Z. *Eupolemus*, Cincinnati, 1974

—*The Dawn of Qumran*, Cincinnati, 1983

Weinfeld, M. 'מגילת־המקדש או תורה למלך', *Shnaton* 3 (1978-79), 214-37

—'The Royal Guard According to the Temple Scroll', *RB* 87 (1980), 394-96

Yadin, Y. 'The Temple Scroll', *BA* 30 (1967), 135-39

—'The Temple Scroll', in *Jerusalem Throughout the Ages* (Hebr.), Jerusalem, 1969, 72-87

—'Temple Scroll', in *Encyclopedia Judaica*, XV, 1971, 996-98

—'Pesher Nahum (4QpNahum) Reconsidered', *IEJ* 21 (1971), 1-12

—'The Temple Scroll', in D.N. Freedman & J. Greenfield (eds.), *New Directions in Biblical Archaeology*, 1971, 156-66

—'Le Rouleau du Temple', in M. Delcor (ed.) *Qumran*, Paris, 1978, 115-19

—'Is the Temple Scroll a Sectarian Document?', in *Humanizing America's*

Iconic Book: SBL Centennial Addresses, 1980, 153-69

— 'Is the Temple Scroll a Sectarian Work?', in *Thirty Years of Archaeology in Eretz-Israel, 1948-1978*, Jerusalem, 1981

Architecture

General

Andrae, W. *Das Gotteshaus und die Urformen des Bauens im Alten Orient*, Berlin, 1930

Badawy, A. *Architecture in Ancient Egypt and the Near East*, Cambridge, Mass., 1966.

Berve, H. and Gruben, G. *Tempel und Heiligtümer der Griechen*, Munich, 1978

Busink, T. A. *Der Tempel von Jerusalem von Salomo bis Herodes* I, *Der Tempel Salomos*, Leiden, 1970; II, *Von Ezechiel bis Middot*, Leiden, 1980

Cohen, R. 'Excavations at Avdat, 1977', *Qadmoniot* 13 (1980), 44-46

Collart, P. & Vicari, J. *Le Sanctuaire de Baalshamin à Palmyre, 1-2: Topographie et Architecture*, Rome, 1969

Coulton, J.J. *The Architectural Development of the Greek Stoa*, London, 1977

Cichy, B. *Baukunst der alten Hochkulturen*, Essen, 1965

Davey, C.J. 'Temples of the Levant and the Buildings of Solomon', *Tyndale Bulletin* 31 (1980), 107-46

Dinsmoore, W.B. *The Architecture of Ancient Greece*, London, 1965

Doxiadis, C.A. *Architectural Space in Ancient Greece*, London, 1977

Ebert, F. *Fachausdrücke des griechischen Bauhandwerks, 1. Der Tempel*, Diss. Würzburg, 1910

Egli, E. *Geschichte des Städtebaus* I, Zürich/Stuttgart, 1959 (1977[2])

Eissfeldt, O. *Tempel und Kulte syrischer Städte in hellenistisch-römischer Zeit*, Leipzig, 1941

Frankfort, H. *The Art and Architecture of the Ancient Orient*, Harmondsworth, 1969[4]

— *Arrest and Movement*, New York, 1978[2]

Fyve, T. *Hellenistic Architecture*, Rome, 1965[2]

Galling, K. *Biblisches Reallexikon*, Tübingen, 1977[2]

Gawlikowski, M. *Le temple palmyrénien*, Warsaw, 1973

Gordon, H.L. 'The Basilica and the Stoa in Early Rabbinical Literature', *The Art Bulletin* 13 (1931), 353-75

Grenier, J.-C. 'Temples ptolémaiques et romains', in *Répertoire bibliographique*, Cairo, 1979

Heinrich, E. *Die Tempel und Heiligtümer im alten Mesopotamien*, 2 vols., Berlin, 1982

Iversen, E. *Canon and Proportion in Egyptian Art*, Warminster, 1973[2]

Kleiner, G. *Die Ruinen von Milet*, Berlin, 1968

Krencker, D. and Zschietzschmann, W. *Römische Tempel in Syrien*, 2 vols., Berlin, 1938 (repr. 1978)

Knell, H. *Grundzüge der griechischen Architektur*, Darmstadt, 1980

Lavas, G.P. *Altgriechisches Temenos: Baukörper und Raumbildung*, Basel, 1974

Lloyd, S., Müller, H.W. and Martin, R. *Architecture de l'Antiquité*, Paris, 1980

MacDonald, W.L. *The Architecture of the Roman Empire* I, *An introductory study*, New Haven, 1982

MacQuitty, W. *Island of Isis. Philae, temple of the Nile*, London, 1976

Major, M. *Geschichte der Architektur* I, Berlin/Budapest, 1976[2]

McEwan, G.J.P. *Priest and Temple in Hellenistic Babylonia*, Wiesbaden, 1981

Müller, W. and Vogel, G. *dtv-Atlas zur Baukunst* I, München, 1977[2]

Mussche, H.F. *Greek Architecture* I, *Religious Architecture*, Leiden, 1968; II, *Civil and Military Architecture*, Leiden, 1963

Netzer, E. *An architectural and archaelogical analysis of building in the Herodian period at Herodium and Jericho* (Hebr.), Diss. Jerusalem, 1977

Oikonomides, A.N. *The Two Agoras in Ancient Athens*, Chicago, 1964

Oren, E. '"Migdol"-Fortresses in Northwestern Sinai', *Qadmoniot* 10 (1977), 71-76

Ragette, F. *Baalbek*, New Jersey, 1980

Rohde, E. *Pergamon—Burgberg und Altar*, Munich, 1982[2]

Rowe, A. *Discovery of the Famous Temple and Enclosure of Serapis at Alexandria*, Cairo, 1946

Sauneron, N. *Temples ptolémaiques et romains d'Egypte*, Cairo, 1956

—and Stierlin, H. *Derniers temples d'Egypte, Edfou et Philae*, Paris, 1975

Schede, M. *Die Ruinen von Priene*, Berlin, 1964

Scully, V. *The Earth, the Temple, and the Gods. Greek Sacred Architecture*, London, 1980[2]

Segal, A. *Stadtplanung im Altertum*, Cologne, 1979

—'Tadmor/Palmyra', *Qadmoniot* 14 (1981), 2-14

Seidl, E.H. & U. 'Grundrisszeichnungen aus dem Alten Orient', *Mitteilungen der deutschen Orientgesellschaft* 98 (1967), 24-45

Seyrig, H., Amy, R. & Will, E. *Le temple de Bel à Palmyre*, 2 vols., Paris, 1968-75

Stern, E. *The Material Culture of the Land of the Bible in the Persian Period, 538-332 B.C.*, Warminster, 1982

—'The Excavations at Tell Mevorach and the Late Phoenician Elements in the Architecture of Palestine', *BASOR* 225 (1977), 17-27

Taylor, G. *The Roman Temples of Lebanon*, Beirut, 1967

Vallois, R. *L'Architecture hellénique et hellénistique à Delos* I, Paris, 1944; II, Paris, 1979

Wetzel, F. *Die Stadtmauern von Babylon*, Leipzig, 1930 (repr. 1967)
—and Weissbach F.H. *Das Hauptheiligtum des Marduk in Babylon, Esagila und Etemenaki*, Leipzig, 1938 (reprint 1967)
Wiegand, T. *Baalbek*, 3 vols., Berlin, 1921-25 (repr. 1973)

The Temple of Jerusalem
Busink, T.A. *Der Tempel von Jerusalem von Salomo bis Herodes* I, *Der Tempel Salomos*, Leiden, 1970; II, *Von Ezechiel bis Middot*, Leiden, 1980 (with abundant bibliographies)
Fritz, V. 'Der Tempel Salomos im Licht der neueren Forschung', *Mitteilungen der deutschen Orientgesellschaft* 112 (1980), 53-68
Haran, M. *Temples and Temple Service in Ancient Israel*, Oxford, 1978
Mazar, B. *The Mountain of the Lord*, Garden City, 1975
Simons, J. *Jerusalem in the Old Testament*, Leiden, 1952
Vincent, L.-H. & Steve, A.M. *Jérusalem de l'Ancien Testament* II, Paris, 1956
Watzinger, C. *Denkmäler Palästinas* II, Leipzig, 1935

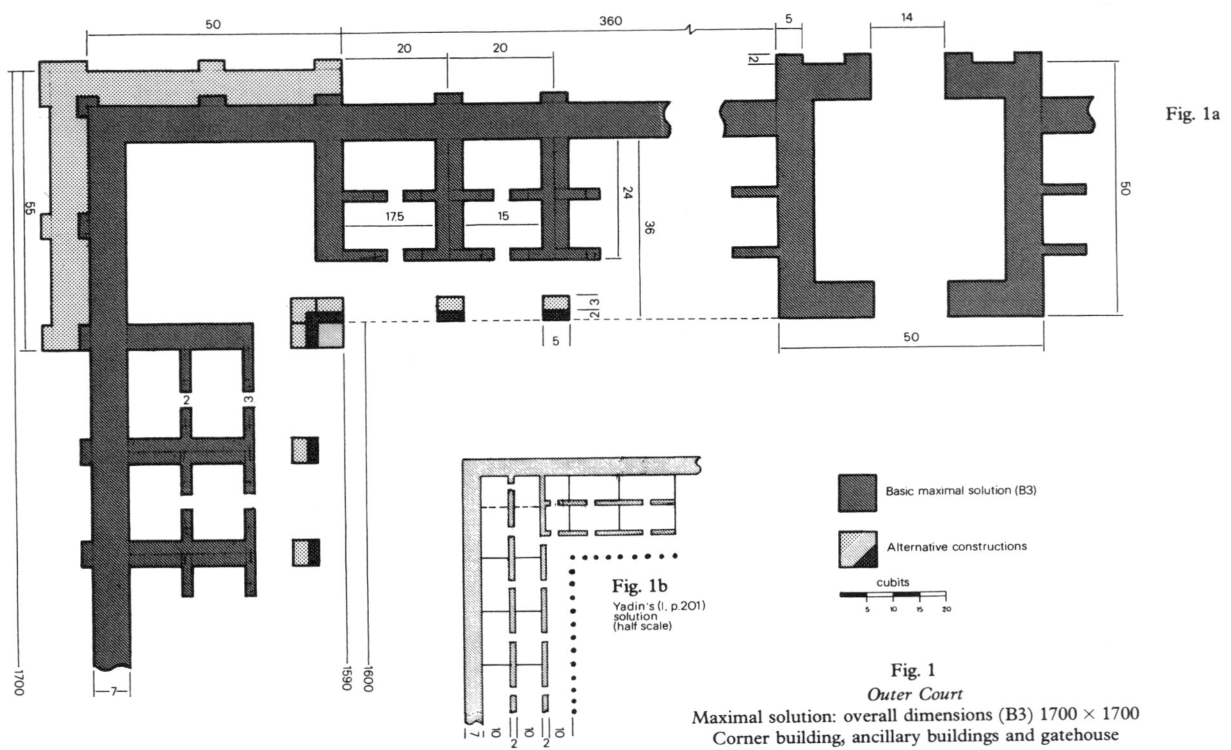
Fig. 1a
50
360
5
14
20
20
2
55
17.5
15
24
36
50
2
3
2 3
5
50
7
1590
1600
1700
Fig. 1b
Yadin's (I, p.201) solution (half scale)
7
10
2
10
2
10
Basic maximal solution (B3)
Alternative constructions
cubits
5
10
15
20

Fig. 1

Outer Court

Maximal solution: overall dimensions (B3) 1700 × 1700

Corner building, ancillary buildings and gatehouse

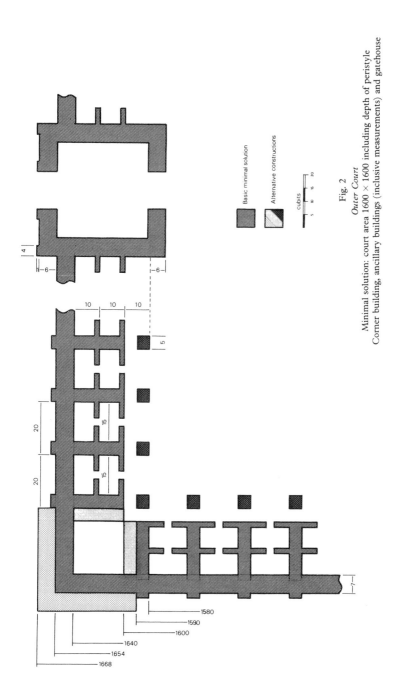

Fig. 2
Outer Court
Minimal solution: court area 1600 × 1600 including depth of peristyle
Corner building, ancillary buildings (inclusive measurements) and gatehouse

Basic minimal solution

Alternative constructions

cubits
5   10   15   20

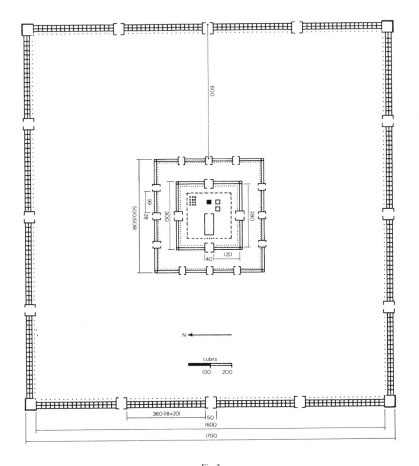

Fig. 3

Overall plan of temple
(Outer court according to maximal solution)

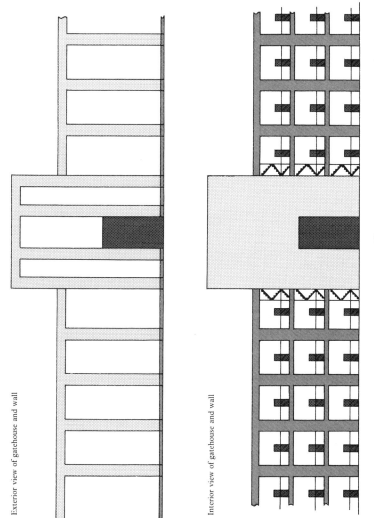

Exterior view of gatehouse and wall

Interior view of gatehouse and wall

Fig. 4

JOURNAL FOR THE STUDY OF THE OLD TESTAMENT
Supplement Series